# RECLAIM

# YOUTH AT RISK

## OUR HOPE FOR THE FUTURE

LARRY K. BRENDTRO
MARTIN BROKENLEG
STEVE VAN BOCKERN

Solution Tree | Press

a division of

Solution Tree

555 North Morton Street
Bloomington, IN 47404
800.733.6786 (toll free) / 812.336.7700
FAX: 812.336.7790

email: info@solution-tree.com
solution-tree.com

Cover photograph by Frankie, a student in the McKinney Homeless Education Project, Sioux Falls, SD

Native American art by George Blue Bird

Printed in the United States of America

ISBN 978-1-879639-86-7

# Table of Contents

Dedication . . . . . . . . . . . . . . . . . . . . . . . . . . . . . . . . . . . . . . . . . v

About the Authors . . . . . . . . . . . . . . . . . . . . . . . . . . . . . . vii

Foreword: Our Hope for the Future
     by Archbishop Desmond Tutu . . . . . . . . . . . . . . . . . . . . . ix

Introduction: The Century of the Child . . . . . . . . . . . . . . . 1

Part I: The Seeds of Discouragement . . . . . . . . . . . . . . . . . . . 7
     Destructive Relationships . . . . . . . . . . . . . . . . . . . . . . . . 9
     Climates of Futility . . . . . . . . . . . . . . . . . . . . . . . . . . . . 15
     Learned Irresponsibility . . . . . . . . . . . . . . . . . . . . . . . . 25
     The Loss of Purpose . . . . . . . . . . . . . . . . . . . . . . . . . . . 34

Part II: The Circle of Courage . . . . . . . . . . . . . . . . . . . . . . . 43
     The Spirit of Belonging . . . . . . . . . . . . . . . . . . . . . . . . 46
     The Spirit of Mastery . . . . . . . . . . . . . . . . . . . . . . . . . . 49
     The Spirit of Independence . . . . . . . . . . . . . . . . . . . . . . 52
     The Spirit of Generosity . . . . . . . . . . . . . . . . . . . . . . . . 57
     Mending the Broken Circle . . . . . . . . . . . . . . . . . . . . . . 60

Part III: The Reclaiming Environment . . . . . . . . . . . . . . . . . 69
     Relating to the Reluctant . . . . . . . . . . . . . . . . . . . . . . . 71
     Brain-Friendly Learning . . . . . . . . . . . . . . . . . . . . . . . . 91
     Discipline for Responsibility . . . . . . . . . . . . . . . . . . . . 103
     The Courage to Care . . . . . . . . . . . . . . . . . . . . . . . . . . 119

Afterword: Honoring George Blue Bird . . . . . . . . . . . . . . . 131

Endnotes . . . . . . . . . . . . . . . . . . . . . . . . . . . . . . . . . . . . . . . 139

Index . . . . . . . . . . . . . . . . . . . . . . . . . . . . . . . . . . . . . . . . . . 155

# Dedication

We dedicate this book to our families, and in particular to
Janna, Daniel, Steven, and Nola Brendtro
Sarah, Anna, and Nic Brokenleg
Mary, Matt, Maggie, and in memory of Catie Van Bockern

# About the Authors

**Dr. Larry Brendtro** is president of Reclaiming Youth International, a nonprofit organization networking those serving children who are in conflict with family, school, and community. Dr. Brendtro has had broad experience as a psychologist, educator, and youth worker and is past president of Starr Commonwealth in Michigan and Ohio. He holds a Ph.D. from the University of Michigan and has served on the faculty of Augustana College, the University of Illinois, and Ohio State University. His publications have been translated in several languages, and he has trained professionals worldwide. Dr. Brendtro is a member of the coordinating council on Juvenile Justice and Delinquency Prevention chaired by the U.S. Attorney General. He was recently adopted into the Lakota tribe and given the name Mato Mani (Walking Bear).

**Dr. Martin Brokenleg** is professor of Native American Studies at Augustana College and dean of the Black Hills Seminars on youth at risk. He holds a doctorate in psychology and is a graduate of the Episcopal Divinity School. He has been a director of The Neighborhood Youth Corps, chaplain in a correctional setting, and has extensive experience as an alcohol counselor. Dr. Brokenleg has consulted and led training programs throughout North America and in Hawaii, New Zealand, and South Africa. He is the father of three children and an enrolled member of the Rosebud Sioux Tribe practicing the culture of his Lakota people. He has taught at Augustana since 1974 and is a recipient of the Orin Lofthus Distinguished Professor award.

**Dr. Steve Van Bockern** is professor of Education at Augustana College and dean of the Reclaiming Youth Institute, which conducts research on strength-based prevention and intervention. Drawing on his experience as a public school principal and teacher at the elementary and secondary levels, Dr. Van Bockern consults with numerous schools and alternative education programs throughout North America. He has directed grants for the National Science Foundation and the Kellogg Foundation and has developed programs for talented students. Dr. Van Bockern serves as a co-director for the Black Hills Seminars and is a senior trainer for the Life Space Crisis Intervention Institute of Hagerstown, Maryland.

The authors can be contacted at Reclaiming Youth, Post Office Box 57, Lennox, SD 57039, www.reclaiming.com, or e-mail: courage@reclaiming.com.

# Our Hope for the Future

## by Archbishop Desmond Tutu

Children from difficult circumstances need someone to throw them a lifeline since it is very difficult to pull oneself up by one's own boot strings. Without help, too many young persons will drop out of school, become involved in substance abuse, and increase the population in jails. We talk about youth with problems as if they are statistics, but they are not statistics. Perhaps we should ask, "What would you do if this was *your* child?"

We seem to have forgotten that people matter more than things. We have given our children ethical values that say, "Whatever you do is all right as long as you don't get caught." We have taught them that success is everything, no matter how ruthless you might be in achieving your results. We have based our whole society on power, portraying compassion, gentleness, and caring as "sissy" qualities. Tough, macho—this is how you should operate. Children adopt these values because they are so prevalent.

I fear that our wonderful expressions of concern for young people are often just so much baloney. This is all hot air because our deeds speak far more eloquently than words. Innovative programs that could provide role models to youngsters who might not have them are jeopardized by a lack of resources. We must realize that it is a very, very shortsighted policy if we fail to redeem and salvage our most needy young people.

A great deal of violence happens among young persons who feel that their lives will end in a cul-de-sac. They may come from depressed communities and lack father figures or caring adults. Without human comforts and outlets for wholesome recreation, they may turn to drugs for excitement and seek status or security in guns and knives. They desperately want to count but take shortcuts to gaining respect. If you can't be recognized for doing good, maybe people will take notice of you if you are troublesome.

We must surmount the "us and them" syndrome and learn to treat each person as part of our family. People who feel marginalized can upset the apple cart. In my country, we have been very fortunate that efforts were made to be as inclusive as possible. We have sought to be nonconfrontational, to make accommodations, to find consensus, and to seek reconciliation and healing. We must all be able to say, "The future is ours." But the future depends so much on the past, and we must heal our memories. We must open the wounds to cleanse them, because if we just close them up and pretend they're not there, they will fester.

God created us as family and this does not mean just our biological family or our community. Ultimately our family includes all of God's children around the world. We ought to be saying, "We have a deep reverence for you, little one, because even though you may be a problem, you are a God-carrier. You belong to God." Each of God's children has a preciousness that cannot be measured. If we don't do all we can to salvage these children, it is almost like spitting in the face of God.

We must look on children in need not as problems but as individuals with potential to share if they are given the opportunity. Even when they are really troublesome, there is some good in them, for, after all, they were created by God. I would hope we could find creative ways to draw out of our children the good that is there in each of them.

# The Century of the Child

Absolutely new truths are very rare. Truths which were once new must be constantly renewed by being pronounced again from the depths of the ardent personal convictions of a new human being.

—Ellen Key[4]

At the dawn of the 1900s, Swedish sociologist Ellen Key[4] prophesied that the world was about to embark on a new era which would be known as "the century of the child." There was great faith that the progress of science would lead to a rebirth of human values and that the education of children would become the highest function of the nation.

Today, with hindsight, one would be unlikely to find a serious scholar who would describe the twentieth century in those terms. The optimism of Key was supplanted by profound ambivalence and even cynicism. Fritz Redl[7] suggested a more apt title for a book on such times in his phrase "Love of Kids, Neglect of Children, Hatred of Youth."

A colleague of ours in computer science observes that his field periodically surges forward following some new "step-jump in technology." Sometimes this is a totally original invention, but often it is the novel recombination of previously existing knowledge. Unfortunately, such step-jumps are seldom found in the behavioral sciences.

Urie Bronfenbrenner[1] characterizes much of recent psychological research as the study of strange behavior in unnatural settings in the trivial pursuit of fragmented knowledge. Our field seems to be caught in a dilemma where those who research and write do not understand practice while gifted practitioners do not believe they have the time or talent to write.

There has been a growing interest in building theories from successful practice rather than just trying to put theory into practice. Psychologist David Hunt[2] challenged researchers to get their "little professor" under control and abandon the pompous notion that "in the beginning there was a blackboard" in favor of the idea that "in the beginning there was experience." There are signs of a renewed respect for the importance of "practice wisdom" in building a knowledge base of professional child and youth work. In the field of education, researchers are investigating characteristics of outstanding schools in order to develop models for effective practice.

Children have been a challenge to their elders since the beginning of time, so perhaps there are few totally novel ideas about how to deal with them. But John Stuart Mill[6] once observed that original thinkers are those who have known most thoroughly what has been thought by their predecessors. In this book we have sought to rediscover the maps used by our forbears as we prepare to sail away from conventional shores. North American philosophies of education and child care have been strongly influenced by the European tradition.[3] In this book we will pursue this transcontinental journey by employing the wisdom of youth work pioneers in the European tradition as well as the untapped heritage of Native American philosophies of child rearing. These theories of practice will be used to guide us through the sea of child development research as we chart a course for reclaiming youth at risk.

We were uncertain what we should call the young people who are the focus of this book, and so we have used different descriptors depending on the focus of discussion. The concept of "at risk," although very broad, avoids blaming the child and points our attention toward the environmental hazards that need to be addressed. We have used the terms "alienated" and "troubled" to emphasize what it feels like to be alone and in conflict. Adults often view these youth as "difficult" to work with and "reluctant" to accept help. The word "reluctant" is unique in the English language because it conveys dual meanings of avoidance and resistance, the prototype responses of persons in conflict. Because we are uncomfortable with most labels, our only excuse for using the foregoing terms is that all of us at some times qualify for such designations.

In contrast, we are pleased with our discovery of the concepts of "courage" and "discouragement." Of course this "discovery" is as original as that of Columbus, who also stumbled upon what was already there. Courage has long been seen as a key virtue in both Western and Native American thought.[9] Dis-couragement also seems to have been well understood by existential philosophers long before Alfred Adler and others in the twentieth century established its importance in child psychology.

The concept of "reclaiming" was first articulated by Martin Wolins, a sociologist at the University of California, Berkeley. The reclaiming environment is one that creates changes that meet the needs of both the young person and the society. To reclaim is to recover and redeem, to restore value to something that has been devalued. Among the features of powerful "reclaiming" environments are these:

1. Experiencing belonging in a supportive community, rather than being lost in a depersonalized bureaucracy.

2. Meeting one's needs for mastery, rather than enduring inflexible systems designed for the convenience of adults.

3. Involving youth in determining their own future, while recognizing society's need to control harmful behavior.

4. Expecting youth to be caregivers, not just helpless recipients overly dependent on the care of adults.[10]

With increasing pressures to serve at-risk youth, schools are assigned responsibility for educating society's most difficult youngsters. These students are found at every point on a "continuum" of services—in regular classrooms, special education programs, alternative schools, and in residential schools and treatment centers. Youth at risk have a right to the "least restrictive" intervention appropriate to their needs. But the ultimate test of the appropriateness of any placement, program, or policy is whether it serves to create the "most reclaiming" environment.

It is no secret what kind of environments lead to "rotten outcomes" with vulnerable youth. Research tells us, two centuries of wisdom from educational pioneers tell us, the children tell us. As Lisbeth Schorr[8] observes, until very recently children who were culturally different, disturbed, learning handicapped, or experiencing trouble at home were simply shoved out of the way because someone in authority decided they did not need or deserve a serious education. By moving aside in large numbers, these children helped a supposedly democratic and universal public school system maintain the facade that it was working smoothly.

But today, we have a greater stake in achieving school success for all of our children. The costs of supporting our dropouts and dumpouts as illiterate, unemployable, violent, or mentally ill citizens are staggering. We no longer can afford the economic drain of disposable people. The youth we are casting aside today are part of a small generation who will have to support a large cohort of retired citizens as the twenty-first century unfolds. We are literally abandoning the persons whom we will ask to support us in retirement.

The outline of this book is straightforward. Part I examines the alienation of children in the oftentimes inhospitable ecology of modern society. Part II presents a holistic Native American philosophy of child development that emerged from the wisdom of peoples who, to use the words of Ellen Key, saw the education of children as the highest function of the nation. Part III highlights the principles and strategies for creating reclaiming environments.

The interdisciplinary nature of our discussion is a reflection of our different but complementary academic backgrounds. In our effort to blend "practice into theory," we have drawn from the enduring wisdom of two of the world's great cultural traditions. For our sense of what is important and "true" in the real world of practice, we are indebted to those courageous and potentially courageous children and families who have shared their life challenges with us. These include students from the Starr Commonwealth Schools in Michigan and Ohio, from public schools in South Dakota and Minnesota, and from the Great Sioux Nation.

Finally, our book is small, following the pattern first proposed by pioneering Polish youth worker Janusz Korczak:[5]

> This book is designed to be as short as possible because it is addressed primarily to a young colleague, who, suddenly thrown into the whirlpool of the most difficult educational problems, the most involved conditions of life, and now

stunned and resentful, has sent out a cry for help.

A fatigued person cannot study thick volumes on education at night. One who is unable to get enough sleep will be incapable of implementing the precious principles he has learned. This shall be brief so that your night's rest may not be spoiled.

PART I

# The Seeds of Discouragement

To be alienated is to lack a sense of belonging,
to feel cut off from family, friends, school or
work—the four worlds of childhood.

—Urie Bronfenbrenner[6]

Developmental psychologist Urie Bronfenbrenner[6] observes
that the gulf between young people and adults in modern society has reached alarming proportions. At the center of these
profound changes is the family under pressure. Parents are too
stressed, schools are too impersonal, and the community is too
disorganized to fulfill the most basic human need of children to
belong. Estranged from family, friends, school, or productive
work, the seeds of discouragement have been sown in the four
worlds of childhood.

Alienated children and youth are assigned a multitude of
labels, most of them unfriendly. They are described as aggressive or anxious, as attention-disordered or affectionless, as
unmotivated or unteachable, as drug abusers or dropouts. Most
terms are either overtly hostile or covertly patronizing in the
long- established tradition of blaming the victim. While professional pejoratives may sound more elegant than labels invoked
by the public, both are often equally condescending.

In Part I we provide an alternative perspective on alienation among children and adolescents. Insofar as possible, we will attempt to shift the focus away from negative *traits* of troubled children, concentrating instead on the *transactions* within their environments. Specifically, we will address four ecological hazards in the lives of youth at risk. These are:

1. DESTRUCTIVE RELATIONSHIPS, as experienced by the rejected or unclaimed child, hungry for love but unable to trust, expecting to be hurt again.

2. CLIMATES OF FUTILITY, as encountered by the insecure youngster, crippled by feelings of inadequacy and a fear of failure.

3. LEARNED IRRESPONSIBILITY, as seen in the youth whose sense of powerlessness may be masked by indifference or defiant, rebellious behavior.

4. LOSS OF PURPOSE, as portrayed by a generation of self-centered youth, desperately searching for meaning in a world of confusing values.

Our discussion of these ecological hazards will be illustrated by four "profiles in discouragement." These profiles are examples drawn from the four worlds of childhood as identified by Bronfenbrenner: family, school, peers, and work. To meet the needs of youth at risk, one must be clear about both the nature of alienation and its locus in the life space of the child.

# Destructive Relationships

Consider these children to have fallen among thieves, the thieves of ignorance and sin and ill fate and loss. Their birthrights were stolen. They have no belongings.

—Karl Menninger[23]

World-renowned psychiatrist Karl Menninger,[23] founder of the Menninger Clinic in Topeka, Kansas, spent his "retirement years" in a second career serving homeless children. Well into his 90s, he advocated the cause of children without belongings. He saw "mistreated, abandoned, rejected, wounded children" as growing in environments where the seeds of discouragement had been planted. As these children develop, they encounter increasing difficulties in social and emotional adjustment. Their lives become "flowers of evil" marked by mental illness, delinquency, depression, and defeat.

When caretakers fail to meet a child's most basic needs, the child learns that they are unpredictable or unreliable. Some children reach beyond their families in search of substitute attachments with other adults or peers. Those more seriously damaged become "relationship-resistant," viewing even friendly, helpful adults with deep distrust. Expecting rejection, they employ protective behaviors learned in prior encounters with threatening persons.[35] The following story of Richard Cardinal shows the depth of relationship hunger in such a child, and the tragic failure of traditional approaches to reclaim alienated youth.

# Profile in Discouragement: A Psychological Orphan

Richard Cardinal was removed from his alcoholic parents at about the time most children were starting school. A Metis Indian from Canada, he and his siblings were dispersed to foster care, generally with white families. His short life would teach much about the indifference of people as he spent 13 years being shunted to a seemingly endless string of homes, schools, youth shelters, and treatment facilities. Each time he was moved was like pulling a piece of used tape from a wall and trying to fasten it again. Before long he seemed to have lost all ability to build close attachments with adults in his life. In a few placements he was reunited with his brother and sister, but when he had to leave them again, he was shattered by the pain of separation.

An intelligent, thoughtful youth, Richard withdrew into himself and began expressing his loneliness in a diary. School teachers were not successful in reaching out to him or cultivating his talent. He began to describe himself as "an outcast" and his frustration would occasionally break through in some act of desperation. He ran away, heading for the North like a salmon swimming upstream to its place of origin. He stole a car, shot a cow, and several times he made attempts at suicide. Once he was found sitting in front of a 7–11 store bleeding from the wrists. Another time he was curled in a dog house with "please help me" written in his own blood. Finally, cut off from human bonds, failing in school, powerless to control his life, overwhelmed with feelings of worthlessness, Richard Cardinal, age 17, hanged himself from a board suspended between two birch trees at his last foster home.

Richard would have been just another marginal person whose death attracted no more attention than his life, except for a powerful documentary produced by The National Film Board of Canada.[27] The film captured the attention of a nation that failed to give him that attention he desperately needed. These excerpts from Richard Cardinal's diary reveal the magnitude of the loneliness in this magnificently sensitive youth:

> I had four hours before I would leave my family and friends behind. I went into the bedroom and dug out my old harmonica. I went down to the barn-yard and sat on the fence. I began to play real slow and sad-like for the occasion, but halfway though the song my lower lip began to quiver and I knew I was going to cry. And I was glad so I didn't even try to stop myself. I guess that my foster mother heard me and must have come down to comfort me. When she put her arm around me, I pulled away and ran up the roadway.

> I didn't want no one to love any more. I had been hurt too many times. So I began to learn the art of blocking out all emotions and shut out the rest of the world. The door would open to no one.

> I'm skipping the rest of the years because it continues to be the same. I want to say to people involved in my life, don't take this personally. I just can't take it any more.

> Love can be gentle as a lamb or ferocious as a lion. It is something to be welcomed, it is something to be afraid of. It is good and bad, yet people live, fight, die for this. Somehow people can cope with it. I don't know. I think I would not be happy with it, yet I am depressed and sad without it. Love is very strange.

## Children without Belongings

There is widespread concern that contemporary society is creating a growing number of children at risk for relationship impairments. Today, the typical child is reared by a single parent or by parents who both work outside the home. The decline of extended families and intimate neighborhoods leaves an isolated nuclear family. Public policy has not kept pace with the reality that one or two unsupported adults are often unequipped to successfully rear their young.

Theologian Martin Marty of the University of Chicago observes that as crucial as the family is to preserving civilization, it has always been the "tribe" rather than the nuclear family that ultimately ensures cultural survival. Throughout history, biological parents have often been unreliable. They were too immature or irresponsible, and many would die while children were still young, but the tribe would nourish the new generation.

It is of the highest imperative that the modern family be strengthened and stabilized. But, in any culture, there will always be a large number of children born to adults whose parenting skills and resources are not sufficient to meet their needs. Contemporary communities cannot avoid their "tribal" responsibilities for those youth at risk. Clearly all sectors of the community have resources to bring to this problem, including religious, social, business, and educational organizations. Whether educators are ready for this responsibility or not, they clearly must play a leading role in responding to the needs of children adrift.

In every city and hamlet, schools could become the new "tribes" to support and nurture children and adolescents at risk. The school is the only institution providing ongoing, long-term relationships with all of our young. Some children spend only minutes a day in conversation with parents, but all are required by law to be in extended contact with the adults who staff our schools. Educators have not yet risen to such challenges, and too often the school itself is a potent breeding ground for further alienation.

If one looks at the structure of a traditional large urban school, one sees that intimate primary relationships have been supplanted by an impersonal bureaucracy. Students and teachers do not relate to one another as whole persons, but in narrow circumscribed roles. Communication is restricted to what one can and must do in a 50-minute hour where a highly structured setting is a sanction against all but teacher-directed behavior. The only spontaneity is the too-frequent disruption, and the only "we" feeling likely to develop is the "we against they" which divides students and teachers into separate camps. Research shows that at each progressive level of the education system, relationships increasingly lack meaning and personal satisfaction.[4] Not surprisingly, students at greatest risk of dropping out of school are those who have never been friends with any teacher.

Nowhere is the critical mass of youth at risk greater than in the inner cities of large metropolitan areas. In a profound analysis of the "truly disadvantaged," William Julius Wilson[39] describes the explosion of a whole range of problems including delinquency, addiction, welfare dependence, family dissolution, out-of-wedlock parenting, and school failure. With the flight of productive role models—both white and black—entire communities are alienated from the mainstream of society. Teen mothers become heads of households because teen fathers lack the social and educational skills needed in marriageable partners. There are few role models for stable lifestyles, as children are socialized by child-parents and their peers.

Rousseau once said, "There are no longer fathers, mothers, children, brothers or sisters. They all hardly know each other.

How could they love each other? Each thinks only of himself. When home is only a sad solitude, one must surely go elsewhere for gaiety."[33] In such cases, the best chances for meaningful human bonds may lie beyond their homes. Hungering for fun and friendship, these children roam the halls of our schools and the streets of our cities in pursuit of meaningful human bonds. The tragedy is that, for many, their only option is to seek out relationships with other outcast and unclaimed youth.

Despite instability within the family, the most formidable influence on the development of children continues to be their parents. Increasingly, education and child welfare policies have mandated parental partnership. However, many professionals who are skillful at building relationships with difficult youth are much less comfortable working with parents.

Professionals and parents are required to "time-share" responsibility for youth at risk, but genuine partnerships are rare. Mutual blaming contests are not. Research shows that parents lodge responsibility first with the school, second with the child, and third with themselves. In contrast, school personnel blame problems first on the home, then on the child, and last on the school.[36] Such contests about problem ownership only intensify the alienation of families and children at risk.

# Climates of Futility

In America they have begun to talk of troubled
children as "throw-away" children. Who can be
less fortunate than those who are thrown away?

— Thom Garfat of Canada to
the South Africa Child Care
Association

Early pioneers in work with difficult youth strongly challenged the indifference and pessimism of their times. They were incurable optimists who could always find cause for hope in the face of the most difficult problems.

Swiss educator Johann Pestalozzi created a castle school for outcast street urchins to demonstrate his revolutionary thesis that "precious hidden faculties" could be found beneath an appearance of ignorance. Jean Marc Itard shocked the intellectuals of Paris by declaring that he could educate a wolf-child, "the wild boy of Aveyron." A century later, Italy's first woman physician, Maria Montessori, advocated the cause of disadvantaged children who were "pinned like mounted butterflies to their desks, spreading their wings of barren and useless knowledge." In the same vein, educator and writer Sylvia Ashton-Warner of New Zealand castigated a lock-step colonial education that enslaved intelligent, resourceful aboriginal children in roles of impotence and inferiority.

In contrast to the outlook of these pioneers, pessimism is commonplace in contemporary approaches to difficult youth. This section discusses how negative environments and expectations can produce failure and futility in young people as well as the adults who share their lives.

## Profile in Discouragement: An Unfriendly School

Much has been written about the importance of positive school climates, but what is known about the kind of climates that are particularly hazardous to vulnerable youth? Much of the educational wisdom on this topic can be summed up in four concepts:

*Negative Expectations:* It has always been a potentially discouraging business to teach difficult children. Two centuries ago, the Swiss educator Pestalozzi gathered a school of brazen, vermin-covered, ignorant, and arrogant street urchins and counseled his teachers to avoid becoming cynical. "The crowning point of education is to convince a child of our fervent love even as we are criticizing him," he declared. Now, a mass of research tells us that negative expectations breed futility in both students and staff.

Our growing understanding of self-fulfilling prophecies or the "Pygmalion effect"[17] should provide abundant warnings about the deleterious effects of pessimistic approaches to children in conflict.

*Punitiveness:* Horace Mann, the leading American educator in the nineteenth century, told teachers they needed to learn to respond to the most difficult pupils like physicians who find challenge in solving difficult cases. To become angry and punish such a child is as illogical as if a surgeon were to attack the limb he is treating. But punishment is coming back into style. Scholarly journals publish articles suggesting that retribution is a respectable means of insuring justice since "an eye for an eye" at least keeps things in perspective. The entire American nation was treated to a movie that conferred knighthood on an urban principal, who, armed with a bullhorn and baseball bat, conquered his petty fiefdom by assaulting and banishing adolescents at risk.

*Boredom:* Jane Addams described urban Chicago youth at the turn of the century as plagued by a lack of adventure; if this were still a coastal nation, one would only have to send difficult youth to sea, and they would return some months later as men. She insisted that most adolescent rebellion today could be remedied by mobilizing the adventurous spirit of youth. Kurt Hahn, founder of the Outward Bound movement, put these ideas into practice in England following the First World War. Still today, in many classrooms the major physical activity is circling answers on a worksheet and the greatest adventure comes from challenging authority.

*Irresponsibility:* "Education is an apprenticeship in responsibility," declared Mann, but this never became more than a clever aphorism. The long, infamous tradition of Western civilization was to treat children as property or vassals or to give lip-service to their status as "future citizens"; all of these attitudes entail deferring real responsibility to adulthood. Pioneer educational psychologist G. Stanley Hall wrote of the powerful idealism of adolescence, and William James proposed harnessing this spirit of service to society as "the moral equivalent of war." But a century later, pollster George Gallup, Jr. ,[15] was reporting that this potential was still untapped as young people were crying, screaming to be used in some demanding task.

## Professional Pessimism

Much current literature on difficult youth is negative, pessimistic, and occasionally even cynical. It is not difficult to locate articles in professional publications in which "experts" gather selective evidence to reinforce their *a priori* views that education or treatment doesn't work, that problem children are likely intellectually or constitutionally defective, or that segregation and punishment are efficient and defensible interventions. Usually biases are considerably more subtle, and not readily noticed unless one has another reference point. Take, for example, the following comparison of descriptions of troubled children:

| From Floyd Starr's 1913 Creed, The Star Commonwealth for Boys: | From a popular professional text on troubled children: |
|---|---|
| "We believe there is no such thing as a bad boy, that badness is not a normal condition but the result of misdirected energy. We believe that every boy will be good if given an opportunity in an environment of love and activity." | "They are abusive, destructive, unpredictable, irresponsible, bossy, quarrelsome, irritable, jealous, defiant—anything but pleasant to be with. Naturally adults choose not to spend time with this kind of child unless they have to." |

The first philosophy reflects an idealism more common before the world wars. Starr's thinking was influenced by experiences in the settlement movement, particularly contacts in Chicago with Jane Addams. The second comes from an otherwise excellent text used to train special educators. While some might argue that this is just idealism versus realism, these are in fact profoundly different ways of looking at the same reality. Floyd Starr remained active until his death in 1979, at 97 years of age. He never abandoned this optimistic cognitive set in spite of six decades of direct work with some of the most difficult youth that could be produced by the streets of Detroit. He frequently criticized the negative attitudes of professionals, accusing them of fostering "deformed schools instead of reformed schools."

An examination of the history of childhood in Western society shows that negative attitudes toward difficult youth are deeply imbedded in the cultural milieu. Pioneers such as Jane Addams and Floyd Starr were not so much products of that culture as antagonists to it. Even today, the predominant patterns of thinking are pessimistic rather than optimistic. This way of thinking fixates on deviance to the exclusion of normality, illness to the exclusion of health. Even highly trained persons have been unable to disengage from the ancient Biblical admonition to stone stubborn sons.

In most fields of professional knowledge, the expert thinks in different ways than the naive observer. But specialists with troubled youth often alter only the words, while the music continues with refrains of "attack" or "avoid." The chart below demonstrates the many commonalities between unsophisticated and professional approaches to difficult children.

The various theories all share the tendency to attribute problems to the troubled individual. Most approaches also embody some forms of coerciveness and avoidance. Such commonalities raise the suspicion that whatever the rationalization, most methods are closely tied to primitive, instinctual responses to threat. Specifically this involves targeting blame and then combatting or disengaging from the noxious individual.

---

## The 10 Ds of Deviance
## in Approaches to Difficult Youth

| Theory | Problem | Typical Responses |
| --- | --- | --- |
| Primitive | Deviant | blame, attack, ostracize |
| Folk Religion | Demonic | chastise, exorcise, banish |
| Biophysical | Diseased | diagnose, drug, hospitalize |
| Psychoanalytic | Disturbed | analyze, treat, seclude |
| Behavioral | Disordered | assess, condition, time out |
| Correctional | Delinquent | adjudicate, punish, incarcerate |
| Sociological | Deprived | study, resocialize, assimilate |
| Social Work | Dysfunctional | intake, case-manage, discharge |
| Educational | Disobedient | reprimand, correct, expel |
| Special Education | Disabled | label, remediate, segregate |

---

From where, then, does this way of thinking about youth come, and why is it so all-pervasive? It is our judgment that the preoccupation with deviance in formal theories is a reflection of powerful underlying naive theories of human behavior.

## Naive Personal Theories of Behavior

Every person is a psychologist. We all relate to one another based on personal theories of human behavior. These theories are products of our unique life experiences as well as innate universal behavioral response tendencies. Heider[21] and other social psychologists have called this the "naive psychology of behavior."

Our personal theories of behavior provide us with a way of making sense of our social world. We develop theories of causality and we attribute characteristics to others, e.g., "he is shiftless, she is courageous." If a person's behavior causes us distress, we are likely to assume the actions were intentional and respond negatively.

Novice youth workers often make the mistake of believing the behavior of a difficult youth is directed at them personally. As they learn to see the behavior as a reflection of the youth's personal needs or distress, they are able to disengage from a knee-jerk response of negativism. This cognitive skill involves perspective-taking or empathy. For example, one's moral reaction to aggression is based on what it looks like from the outsider's vantage point. To the "aggressor," it may seem like self-defense.

Tables 1 and 2 are based on social psychology research in attribution theory, specifically the process of attributing meaning to social behavior. Usually our cognitions, feelings, and behavior are in balance. Thus, negative thoughts are often accompanied by negative feelings and negative actions. It follows that altering

## TABLE 1

## THE IMPACT OF NEGATIVE PERSONAL
## THEORIES OF BEHAVIOR

COGNITION

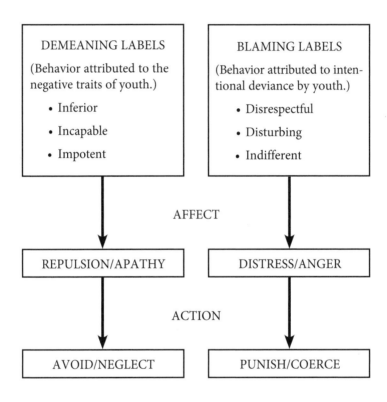

DEMEANING LABELS

(Behavior attributed to the negative traits of youth.)

- Inferior
- Incapable
- Impotent

BLAMING LABELS

(Behavior attributed to intentional deviance by youth.)

- Disrespectful
- Disturbing
- Indifferent

AFFECT

REPULSION/APATHY

DISTRESS/ANGER

ACTION

AVOID/NEGLECT

PUNISH/COERCE

## TABLE 2

## THE IMPACT OF POSITIVE PERSONAL
## THEORIES OF BEHAVIOR

COGNITION

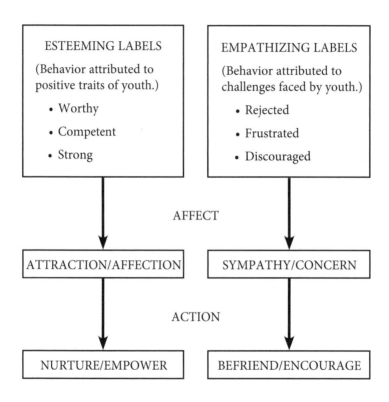

ESTEEMING LABELS

(Behavior attributed to positive traits of youth.)

- Worthy
- Competent
- Strong

EMPATHIZING LABELS

(Behavior attributed to challenges faced by youth.)

- Rejected
- Frustrated
- Discouraged

AFFECT

ATTRACTION/AFFECTION

SYMPATHY/CONCERN

ACTION

NURTURE/EMPOWER

BEFRIEND/ENCOURAGE

any part of the thought/feeling/action triad can have an effect on the other elements. Most social psychology research assumes the following dominant sequence:

$$\text{cognition} \longrightarrow \text{affect} \longrightarrow \text{behavior}$$

According to this view, our thoughts guide our feelings, which provide motivation and direction to our behavior.[38]

Adults working with difficult children have a strong tendency to revert to negative theories of behavior when under stress, because they are more likely to overreact to the child's behavior. Abraham Maslow once suggested that behavior managers select their explanation for behavior in accord with their own generalized optimism or pessimism. Often this negative bias is quite unintentional. For example, a common practice among psychologists and special educators is to employ "behavior check-lists" as a means of assessing the characteristics of challenging children. But, by design, many of these instruments list only negative traits, thereby shifting attention away from the young person's strengths and potentials.

Negative labels assigned to a child's behavior easily taint the child as a person. Some even assert that it is not possible to reject a child's behavior without implicitly rejecting the child.[18] In our experience, it is possible and important to accept the child even while rejecting the behavior.[26] But "moralistic" communication implies superiority of the adult and rejection of the child.

Negative theories of behavior (see Table 1) employ demeaning and blaming labels that lead to negative feeling and actions toward a youngster. Positive theories of behavior (see Table 2) employ esteeming and empathizing labels that foster positive affect and action. Certainly one cannot accurately communicate without resorting to some negative labels. However, successful youth workers are those who can reframe their thinking to foster the positive feelings and actions essential to the helping process.

The German poet and educator Goethe wrote that one must look past the fault to find the "germ of virtue." When "stubbornness" can be recast as "persistence," then a liability becomes a potential asset. Recent policies towards difficult youth are bankrupt of this wisdom from earlier times:

> An administrator of the Office of Juvenile Justice and Delinquency Prevention[30] declared it was his mission to make these "predators" accountable. . . . In bold contrast, Austrian educator August Aichorn in 1925 described delinquents as "wayward youth" searching to satisfy unmet needs for love.

> The Supreme Court of the United States ruled that corporal punishment in the schools and capital punishment of youth over sixteen are not cruel and unusual punishment. . . . The Wandervogel youth movement of the Weimar Republic revolutionized education and youth work with the credo that modern youth are discouraged and punishment only fuels discouragement.

As Goethe also observed, "everything important has been thought of before—the difficulty is to think of it again."

# Learned Irresponsibility

So we suggest you sit quietly, behave yourselves, and study in the schools we provide as a holding pen until we are ready to accept you into the adult world.

—Harold Howe II, Harvard University

One of the most patronizing statements that adults make about youth is that "they are our future citizens." A related myth is that obedience training produces responsible adults. The simple but elusive truth is, to paraphrase W.E.B. Dubois, only responsibility teaches responsibility. Anthropologist Ruth Benedict[3] criticized our culture for excluding youth from responsibility only to blame them for their irresponsibility. The irresponsibility of contemporary youth takes many forms:

- the learned helplessness of those who see themselves as pawns of others
- the defiant rebellion of those struggling to break the chains of authority
- the narcissism of an affluent generation lacking a sense of social responsibility
- the negative peer subcultures of predatory gangs terrorizing our cities

Rousseau[33] cleverly demonstrated in *Emile* how adults unwittingly teach irresponsibility in their attempts to deal with irresponsible children. By training children to be obedient, we teach them to be machines in the hands of others. By punishing rebellion, we teach children to manipulate and deceive to escape authority. Our attempts to satisfy the selfish child teach him to believe that he owns the universe. And we feel impotent in countering the power of peers, for "the lessons pupils get from one another in the schoolyard are a hundred times more useful than everything they will ever be told in class."

## Profile in Discouragement: A Youth Counterculture

Dr. Carlos Canon, an educational psychologist from Bogotá, Colombia, first introduced us to the *"Muchachos de la Calle,"* children of the streets. Called *"gamines,"* these gangs of homeless or runaway children live with their peers as outcasts in one of the most impoverished cities of the world.

Sociologists have studied this youth subculture for generations. The principle cause of *"gaminismo"* is the destruction of family units, and these gangs provide a sense of belonging to youth whose needs are not met by the existing social structure.

A Salesian priest, Father Javier De Nicolo, began a careful study of the culture of these groups, their language, laws, tradition, activities, and relationships. He believed it would only be possible to understand these children of the streets if one shared their habitat, visiting the drug dens and thieves' markets where they plied their trades for survival. Through this process, Father Javier and a team of psychiatrists, psychologists, social workers, educators, and university students were able to create Bosconia La Florida, a network of innovative programs for the *gamines.*[1]

The *gamines,* as young as five or six years old, can be found by day roaming the city in small gangs of peers that are termed *galladad,* literally "flock of roosters." Existing in a climate of almost total freedom, they support themselves by theft and very early are exposed to a wide range of social evils. When night settles upon the city, *gamines* regroup for protection into cross-age living cells called *camadas* or "dens of kittens." Each *camada* is led by *jefe,* an older youth who is a veteran of the streets. Sociologists have been able to map out the precise boundaries of each *camada,* and they are well-organized with all *jefes* reporting to a city-wide *Jefe* of *jefes.*

The *gamines* are at the bottom of the ladder, outcasts in a very hierarchical society. Their mothers couldn't support them, their stepfathers abhor them, schools ignore them, police jail them, and society disowns them. Their role models are lock-pickers and pick-pockets, and they are wary of all adults in authority. One such youth recounted how storekeepers would chase him and his companions away like stray animals if they huddled in the doorway for protection from the weather. The *muchacho de la calle* is the stereotype of youth at risk: distrusted, distrustful, dirty face, unkempt hair, and eyes without hope for the future.

Yet in spite of their problems, those working with the *gamines* are amazed at their camaraderie, their pride, and their sense of independence and group identity. They call one another *nero* (a shortened term for *compañero)* and stand together in fierce loyalty against a hostile world. One cannot help but see a resilience and strength in these youth. The *gamines* are not the only poor children in Bogotá. The child of the streets has not yet given up, only chosen to assert his independence. There is an element of superiority in all of this. Noted Latin American writer Castro Gaycedo[16] writes of the remarkable talents and resourcefulness of the *gamine.* While children of the upper classes are sheltered from the harshness of life (perhaps being groomed to attend college in the United States), the *gamines* must struggle for life itself. Given their choice between enslavement in a pseudo-home and misery with liberty on the streets, the *gamine* has embraced freedom. Any educational approach that undermines this autonomy is destined to failure.

The *gamines* are a variation of negative youth subcultures and gangs that are found throughout the world. Young people who have embraced lifestyles of freedom without responsibility cannot be reclaimed by either permissive or authoritarian approaches. Adults who place no demands on these youth are viewed as weak, and are abandoning them to the tyranny of negative peers. But to demand submission is to fuel rebellion and the rejection of adult values. The formidable challenge is to develop new educational approaches that avoid the pitfalls of either overindulgence or authoritarian obedience.

## The Tyranny of Indulgence

Rousseau[33] observed that the surest way of creating a miserable child was to accustom him to get everything he desires. The child who has only to want in order to receive believes himself to be the owner who regards all others as his slaves. Rousseau believed that it was most important to distinguish between what a child "needed" and what he "wanted." The needs should be richly nourished, but to cater to his every whim was a blueprint for creating a young tyrant. These observations are well-supported by psychological research on the effects of excessive permissiveness. Children from such backgrounds may suffer a variety of problems:

- Self-esteem may be lowered because the child is unsure of what is valued and what behaviors will gain approval.[9]

- Delinquency may be reinforced as adults keep giving "another chance."[7]

- Aggression increases if permissiveness is paired with adult hostility.[31]

Still, it would be incorrect to say that permissive child-care practices in and of themselves place children at risk. For example, there is abundant research evidence that democratic child-rearing techniques foster responsibility and moral development, and that, without a reasonable amount of freedom, a child cannot develop autonomy. Thus, it is an oversimplification to talk about "permissive versus strict" because there are so many other variables that interact with this.

Some adults are not so much permissive as they are indifferent. Their lack of involvement with their child's behavior is a measure of their disinterest in their role as parent, teacher, or counselor. In a real sense of the word, these are "care-less" adults. Such adults will not likely have much influence on youth. Research shows that young people seek help only from adults that they see as caring and nurturing.[4]

Other adults are overwhelmed by their own problems and the difficulty of managing children, and retreat from an active role in the daily life of the child. This pattern is becoming much more common among the large number of unmarried teenage parents. Still children themselves, many of these "premature mothers" lack the social maturity and personal resources to meet the responsibility of parenting.

In some cases, adults may get vicarious satisfaction out of the antics of a child's wild behavior. This is more than permissiveness for they are training a child in mischief or evil. A prominent example in history is the childhood of Louis XIII of France. As a small boy, he was taught sexual tricks that he eagerly performed for the entertainment of adult onlookers. At 14, Louis was married and forcibly put in his wife's bed by his mother while young men gathered around to cheer him on with ribald stories.[13]

Professionals working with abused children often encounter situations where adults have lured the child into substance abuse, theft, or sexual activity. This is seen in Tully's[35] analysis of a child called Rocky as he developed from a sexually abused preschooler to an antisocial teen. Meet Rocky as he enters kindergarten:

> His aggression continued to escalate and he
> acted in an intimidating manner toward his fel-
> low students. . . . His behavior and vocabulary
> indicated a sexual awareness and it was impos-
> sible to keep him away from other children
> in the bathroom. . . . Rocky's mother would
> describe how he called attention to himself in
> a sexual manner by saying, "Look, I'm mastur-
> bating," or "Look, my penis is sticking up." He
> would unbutton her blouse, as he sat on her
> lap, and state, "I want to play with your boo-
> bies." When directed to a task by his mother,
> he would frequently respond with profane
> language, knock over chairs, and throw objects
> at her. His approach to his mother was that of
> a peer; periodically he even demonstrated a
> superiority to her.

In these most severe cases of care-less parenting, children fail to internalize moral values. Seeming to lack conscience or concern for others, such youth are given labels like "psychopathic" or "affectionless." They are among the most difficult children to teach or treat. Often discarded by schools and community, they are cut off from the human bonds that make one human.

## The Tyranny of Obedience

The saga of discipline in Western civilization is a litany of futile attempts to compel the young person to obedient behavior. The consistent strategy has been to control all deviations by punishing or excluding those who violate the rules. For centuries, schools have used elaborate codes of regulations to attempt to instill compliant behavior. However, students have been highly resourceful in circumventing these rigid rules. The records are filled with cases of poultry stealing, snakes in tutors' chambers, drunken frolics, cows in the chapel, and sundry routs and noises. When intolerant masters sought to enforce the codes, the school was in a state of constant tension.[32]

Today, many education and treatment programs carry forward this well-established tradition of coercion and punitiveness.[24] With the advent of scientific management in the nineteenth century, schools became depersonalized bureaucracies, replacing primary human relations with an elaborate system of rules. In a remarkable bit of "newspeak" (i.e., faults are relabeled as virtues), the American Association of School Administrators applauded formal codes of conduct in student handbooks as the "most important innovation of American schools for the control and management of student behavior. . . . The effective code carries a clear message to the student: This you can do; this you cannot do; and if you do what you shouldn't, this is the price you pay."[5]

Nothing that we know about human beings suggests that we have been programmed to be obedient. But Western civilization resounds with the theme that authority is to be revered, and obedience, if not natural, is certainly ideal. Anthropologist Walter Miller[25] of Harvard described what happened when explorers with this old-world view of authority first encountered Native North Americans. Europeans were dumbfounded that obedience was not part of the Indian culture. The observations of various French and English explorers of that time paint a picture of puzzlement:

- Subordination is not a maxim among these savages; the savage does not know what it is to obey.

- This is the reason they always give for it, that one man is as much a master as another, and since all men are made of the same clay, there should be no distinction or superiority among them.

Such independence was not to the liking of European generals who had plans to train militias of Indians to plunder the new continent for their respective crowns. A feasibility study by the French was highly pessimistic, concluding that any captain trying to command a company of Indian soldiers would be told curtly that he should do it himself, which of course would be a very bad example for French troops. The explorers concluded that Indians must have some defect in the capacity for obedience.

The ethnocentric European was imprisoned in a cultural history where the fundamental "bond of society" had always been obedience: vassals obeyed lords, priests obeyed superiors, subjects obeyed kings, slaves obeyed masters, women obeyed men, and children obeyed everybody. Naturally, education and child rearing were heavily influenced by the obedience training model. Not until the time of Rousseau, in the eighteenth century, was serious consideration given to other views.

Rousseau believed it was essential for adults to have influence over children, but not by giving orders. "Let him always believe he is the master, and let it always be you who are." But he attacked the notion that one teaches responsibility by disciplining for obedience. This only teaches them that they must always either obey or command. Children who are docile when little grow up to be dupes as adults.

He argued that children should be trained to be self-sufficient as early as possible. But this should be "well-regulated freedom" designed to give the child abundant opportunity to learn from experience and natural consequences. In this manner, the child who has been given responsibility to make decisions in childhood would become a responsible, disciplined adult. But children subjugated to obedience training would throw off the yoke of authority when no longer under control of the adult.

The concept of obedience training is closely intertwined with the notion that "children should learn to follow rules." While that is not debatable, the important question concerns why children do follow rules. If rules are imposed by external force, children will follow them as long as they are policed. When out of the range of surveillance, anything goes.

# The Loss of Purpose

Millions of children are not safe physically, educationally, economically, or spiritually. . . . The poor black youths who shoot up drugs on street corners and the rich white youths who do the same thing in their mansions share a common disconnectedness from any hope or purpose.

—Marian Wright Edelman[12]
Children's Defense Fund

From the dawn of human history, people have bonded together for mutual protection and support. However difficult existence might have been, the goal of life was to insure the survival of oneself and the tribe. Now, as Victor Frankl[14] noted, the struggle for survival has subsided. The new question becomes "survival for what?" More and more people today have the means to live but no meaning to their existence.

Young people cannot develop a sense of their own value unless they have opportunities to be of value to others. William Shakespeare observed that "it is one of the most beautiful compensations of this life that no man can sincerely help another without helping himself." But in contemporary society, this spirit of mutual caring is often lost in the selfish pursuit of individual goals. The Jeffersonian concept of "life, liberty and the pursuit of happiness" has mutated to a life free of social responsibility in the pursuit of personal gain. Unfortunately, many of our education and treatment programs and even our theories of human behavior support this self-centered irresponsibility.

Two psychologists from Duke University[37] indict the major theories of human psychology as contributing to the destruction of community by promoting selfishness:

> There is currently in our society an enormous emphasis on the self-narcissism, self-concern and preoccupation with "me". . . . A surprisingly broad and influential range of psychological theory turns out to legitimatize selfishness.

Various psychological theories reduce human behavior to hedonism. If people help others, it is for self-reinforcement, or because of an underlying pleasure drive, or because they feel guilty. Even the humanistic goal of self-actualization can mutate into selfishness.

Schools have institutionalized selfish strategies to the detriment of cooperation. Addicted to hyperindividualism and cut-throat competition, schools pit students against one another in the struggle for educational fitness. As in psychology, there are hopeful signs of a course-correction toward cooperation and building communities of caring. This trend must be accelerated, for young people are in desperate need of an antidote to the malaise and antisocial lifestyles that accompany the loss of purpose.

## Profile: Work without Meaning

Writing in *The Prophet,* Kahlil Gibran declared that "work is love made visible." The belief that work is virtuous is deeply rooted in Western culture, and it is a truism that work teaches young people responsibility. But sociologists who have examined the role of work among teenagers come up with a very different and unsettling picture. A job is no longer a rite of passage to adult responsibility, but a way of celebrating the materialism of the selfish society.

In their fascinating book, *When Teenagers Work,* Greenberger and Steinberg[19] document the psychological costs of youth employment. During the first half of the twentieth century, most working teens were contributing productively to supporting their families or saving for future expenses, such as college. Now, most teens make no contribution to family expenses and many do not save. Instead, earnings go for such expenses as cars and stereos, movies and recreation. This distinctively self-centered lifestyle has crept up unnoticed by adults who take for granted the large part-time teen labor force that staffs fast-food counters and cleans motel rooms and office buildings.

Establishments employing teens are typically located in wealthier neighborhoods that are beyond the reach of disadvantaged youth who might really benefit from earnings. While apprenticeships of earlier generations taught a craft by close association with a skilled adult, today's jobs offer little of educational value. Greenberger[19] characterizes these as dead-end, unchallenging "McJobs" in a workplace dominated by uncommitted part-time employees. The assistant manager is often another teen who has been around long enough to know where all the keys fit. Such experiences lay a foundation of attitudes of contempt for the value of work as enjoyable and satisfying.

Work is seriously interfering with education, and the additional stresses are increasing the use of alcohol and other drugs. Parents seem ambivalent about interfering, harboring in their own minds fond memories of how they benefited from work. Child labor laws that have been on the books for generations are often ignored, and teachers have to try to motivate at 8:20 A.M. a youth who has closed the Chicken Joy franchise at midnight the night before. As one teacher asked, "Why is it that the priorities for so many students are (1) job, (2) party, and (3) school?"

Teens with money to blow are easy prey to economic exploitation, and massive advertising campaigns are created to lure them into the hedonism of a materialistic society. Paychecks reward long hours of work with premature affluence, plunging youth into a level of consumption that is inconsistent with the obligations many will have in ensuing years. And, perhaps most serious of all, the many hours spent at work block the opportunity for participation in other more developmentally appropriate activities, making them economically rich but psychologically poor.

All of this is turning theories of delinquency upside down. It once was the poor youth who were at great risk for delinquency, but now affluent teens with plentiful disposable income are also highly vulnerable. Funds from work are used to purchase "wheels" which permit one to escape parental influence in the search for illicit excitement and stress-reducing chemicals. Research[10] demonstrates that the greater the "net worth" of a youth (value of possessions acquired with his own money), the more the youth is at risk for these destructive activities. The work ethic has backfired as money brings consumptive power but not social responsibility.

## The Misery of Unimportance

German educator Kurt Hahn described modern youth as suffering from the "misery of unimportance." In earlier times they were indispensable for the survival of the family unit. Working in the fields and shops beside their elders, they built a life and a nation. Experiences in extended families and cohesive neighborhoods made cooperation an everyday occurrence. The young and the elderly helped one another, and large families offered abundant opportunities to give and receive love.[2]

Today, all of this sounds like a fantasy island. Now cousins are just photographs in an album, and grandma is a three-minute transcontinental call. Our homes are fitted with security devices and our yards are cordoned off with fences to protect ourselves from our neighbors. A school in California secures funds for a concrete wall around its playground to protect children from stray bullets fired by warring gangs in the housing project across the street. Nobody mentions that most of the occupants of the project are also children, since that is on the other side of the wall.

While youth hunger for a feeling of importance, adults infantilize them. The typical approach to the cries of boredom from youth is to build them a new playground or teen-town where they are told to go and play some more.[20] Today, little is asked of young people except that they be consumers. A vast industry serves youth with schooling, entertainment, and goods of all kinds, but there are limited opportunities for the young themselves to produce goods and services for others.[22]

Various national commissions have recommended that young people become involved in community service activities. This is a promising idea, but it raises the question of the amount of time youth are presently allocating for volunteer work. A study by the Search Institute[4] asked 10,000 young adolescents the following question: "Think about the helpful things you have done in the last month—for which you did not get paid, but which you did because you wanted to be kind to someone else." Three-quarters spent less than two hours helping others in the previous month; this includes a third of the young people in the study who said they had done nothing at all. A quarter were involved three or more hours during the previous month. One might conclude from this that volunteer work is not presently a major force in the development of responsibility in contemporary youth.

Deprived of opportunities for genuine productivity, lured into consumptive roles, young people come to believe that their lives make little difference to the world. Those who feel the most powerless develop distorted ways of thinking, which psycholo-

gists label as "external locus of control" or "lack of personal efficacy." They feel like helpless pawns following somebody else's
script, rather than authors who can write the drama of their own
destiny. They believe they are but victims of fate or the whims
of powerful others.

Perhaps the most damaging proof of the child's unimportance is the shrinking amount of attention from adults who "don't
have time." Steve Charleston,[8] a Native American professor of
theology, describes this tyranny of time in Western culture:

> We have been fooled into believing time is real;
> it isn't, of course. It is an invention of the human
> mind for describing change and motion. Not
> until very recently have humans ever tried to
> govern their life activity by numbers generated
> by a tiny machine. The great cycle of seasons and
> of the day, the natural development of growth,
> these were time. The rest is only as real as we
> want it to be. And as demanding.

Charleston reminds us of the many idioms we have invented
to describe something that doesn't exist: We make time, save
time, spend time, waste time, borrow time, budget time, invest
time, and manage time until, in exhaustion, we call time out.

In contrast to time, relationships are real. They exist in
the intimate spaces of our lives where we narrow the distance
between ourselves and others. Family, friendship, community—
these are the bonds of reality.

Today these bonds are being torn apart by the hands of
Western time. We invoke another "time word" to mask the
continued destruction of love in our society: it is called "quality"
time. Now not only are we quantifying time, we are qualifying it.
We are willing into existence the illusion that love can be mea-

sured by seconds or minutes; that "human relationships can be made warm in the microwave of quick encounters."

We cannot care for children in convenient time; we cannot learn from our elders in convenient time; we cannot maintain marriages in convenient time. The result of adjusting our lives to the fiction of time will inevitably be empty adults, lonely elders, and neglected children.

## The Depersonalization of Education

Educators have long been intrigued by principles borrowed from business and industry. In the late nineteenth century, schools began a major transformation by copying the emerging concepts of Taylor's theory of scientific management. This meant retitling the headmaster as "superintendent" just as in a factory and establishing hierarchical, military-like systems of command and control. Labor (viz. teaching) was specialized in the belief that repetitive tasks could be performed more efficiently, and teachers could be interchanged like replaceable parts. The size of schools inexorably expanded in the quest for "economy of scale." Informal problem solving through primary group relationships gave way to layers of management and formal rules and procedures. Experts on school management were ecstatic, as shown by this 1875 account by William Payne:[28] "The world of teaching thus follows the law which prevails in all well-regulated industries. This general movement is characteristic of a growing civilization."

Schools and social service organizations continued to follow the trends from business throughout the twentieth century. The belief was that human service organizations would work better if run like corporations or the military.[11] The craze for data-based management and bottom-line cost efficiency pushed aside traditional human wisdom. Supposedly scientific consultants focused on what was readily measurable, namely splinter skills and microperformances. But then a new wave crashed upon corporate America. The new goal became building quality organizations which were people-oriented.

Research from business pointed to the importance of creating positive organizational cultures. A successful school, like a successful business, is a cohesive community of shared values, beliefs, rituals, and ceremonies. The community celebrates its saga by telling the stories of heroes and heroines who embody the core values of the community. Human bonds are forged to release a powerful synergy of shared responsibility. All members are involved as the adversarial mentality is supplanted by a spirit of cooperation and mutual commitment.

Research on effective schools has shown that a key characteristic of programs that foster good discipline is the creation of a "total school environment" rather than adopting isolated practices to counter behavioral problems.[29] The Israeli sociologist Yochanan Wozner[40] sees educational institutions as powerful environments that transmit adult values to the young. Such values are particularly critical in organizations whose mission is "reclaiming" troubled youth. When schools have such a clear value system (which Wozner calls a "unifying theme"), then all other relationships will become consistent with these shared values. In the following section, we turn our attention to the crucial challenge of creating a shared foundation of values.

# PART II
# The Circle of Courage

They had what the world has lost. They have
it now. . . . Be it for now or a hundred years
from now, or a thousand—so long as the race
of humanity shall survive—the Indian keeps his
gift for us all.

—John Collier[7]

When professionals are told they are expected to build
positive cultures in schools and child-care agencies, they are
often perplexed. Even anthropologists who study cultures were
never taught how to manufacture them. What could constitute
the core of shared values, the unifying theme of such a culture?
When we ask our college students to list what they believe to be
the pre-eminent values in contemporary society, the prominent
mainstay is "success" as defined by wealth, power, and materialistic hedonism. Clearly we will have to look somewhere else if
we are to find a value base appropriate for youth at risk.

Traditional Native American child-rearing philosophies
provide a powerful alternative in education and youth development. These approaches challenge both the European cultural
heritage of child pedagogy and the narrow perspectives of many
current psychological theories. Refined over 15,000 years of
civilization and preserved in oral traditions, this knowledge is

little known outside the 200 tribal languages that cradle the Native Indian cultures of North America.

Indians were conquered by militarily and technologically superior European invaders who saw them as primitive peoples who had much to learn but little to offer to a modern society. In reality, Native peoples possessed profound child psychology wisdom that might well have been adopted by the immigrants to North America. Instead, missionaries and educators set out to "civilize" their young "savages" with an unquestioned belief in the superiority of Western approaches to child care. Typically, children were removed from families and placed in militaristic schools. Forbidden to use their own language under penalty of severe whippings, their supposedly inferior Indian identity was deliberately stripped away.[15] "Kill the Indian to save the child" was the battle cry of white educators. Generations of such cultural intrusion have left deep scars of alienation on Native American children and families.

Native American philosophies of child management represent what is perhaps the most effective system of positive discipline ever developed. These approaches emerged from cultures where the central purpose of life was the education and empowerment of children. Modern child development research is only now reaching the point where this holistic approach can be understood, validated, and replicated.

Fostering self-esteem is a primary goal in socializing all children. Lacking a sense of self-worth, a young person from any cultural or family background is vulnerable to a host of social, psychological, and learning problems.[16] In his definitive work on self-concept in childhood, Stanley Coopersmith[9] observed that four basic components of self-esteem are significance, competence, power, and virtue:

*Significance* is found in the acceptance, attention, and affection of others. To lack significance is to be rejected, ignored, and not to belong.

*Competence* develops as one masters the environment. Success brings innate satisfaction and a sense of efficacy, while chronic failure stifles motivation.

*Power* is shown in the ability to control one's behavior and gain the respect of others. Those lacking power feel helpless and without influence.

*Virtue* is worthiness judged by values of one's culture and of significant others. Without feelings of worthiness, life is not spiritually fulfilling.

Traditional Native educational practices addressed each of these four bases of self-worth: (1) significance was nurtured in a cultural milieu that celebrated the universal need for belonging; (2) competence was ensured by guaranteed opportunities for mastery; (3) power was fostered by encouraging the expression of independence; and (4) virtue was reflected in the pre-eminent value of generosity.

The number four has sacred meaning to Native people who see the person as standing in a circle surrounded by the four directions. Lakota Sioux artist George Blue Bird has portrayed this philosophy of child development in the medicine wheel in the art accompanying the text. We propose belonging, mastery, independence, and generosity as the central values—the unifying theme—of positive cultures for education and youth work programs. We believe the philosophy embodied in this circle of courage is not only a cultural belonging of Native peoples, but a cultural birthright for all the world's children.

# The Spirit of Belonging

Be related, somehow, to every one you know.

—Ella Deloria[10]

In traditional Native society, it was the duty of all adults to serve as teachers for younger persons. Child rearing was not just the province of biological parents, but children were nurtured within a larger circle of significant others. From the earliest days of life, the child experienced a network of caring adults. Standing Bear[35] observed that each child belonged both to a certain family and to the band; wherever it strayed, it was at home, for all claimed relationship.

> The days of my infanthood and childhood were spent in surroundings of love and care. In manner, gentleness was my mother's outstanding characteristic. Never did she, nor any of my caretakers, ever speak crossly to me or scold me for failures or shortcomings.

Kinship in tribal settings was not strictly a matter of biological relationships, but rather a learned way of viewing those who shared a community of residence. The ultimate test of kinship was behavior, not blood: you belonged if you acted like you belonged.[37] Children were trained to see themselves as related to virtually all with whom they had regular contact. They honored valid kinship bonds, and relationships were manufactured for persons still left out so that everyone would feel included in the great ring of relatives.

Treating others as related was a powerful social value that transformed human relationships. Drawing them into one's circle motivated one to show respect and concern, and live with a minimum of friction and a maximum of good will.[10] To this day, one of the similarities among various Indian peoples is a quiet, soft-spoken manner of dealing with others, which results from a world view that all belong to one another and should be treated accordingly.[5]

The sense of belonging extended to nature as well. Animals, plants, people, and streams all were interdependent. From childhood, children were taught through stories that if this harmony was upset, tragedies could result. All are related, and one's actions impinge on the natural environment. Maintaining balanced ecological relationships is a way of ensuring balance in one's own life.[1]

Research shows that belonging to a community (Tiyospaye) continues to be the most significant factor in Sioux identity.[29] This belonging is expressed by vibrant cross-generational relationships such as grandparents sharing stories and legends with children. Community leaders are not isolated but regularly visit Tiyospaye residents and provide counsel when problems arise. The presence of a strong sense of belonging makes young people more receptive to guidance from other community members. Native youth have learned to listen and reflect on advice from concerned adults who approach them in a caring manner. Peer-group controls are also highly effective with Native youth; if a youngster is not responsive to group influence, this is a sure sign that the person does not feel he or she belongs.[16]

The theologian Martin Marty[26] indicated that contemporary civilization is threatened by a loss of the sense of community that characterizes tribal peoples. One Indian summed it up long ago: "You are each a one man tribe." Fortunately, authorities in many disciplines are recognizing this problem. Attention is being given to social support networks of friends, neighborhood, and relatives that can provide enduring patterns of nurturance.[40] There is growing concern about cross-generational alienation and the need to involve elders in child rearing.[4] Educators are seeking to rekindle a sense of shared community and employ cooperative strategies of learning.[18, 33]

The pioneering American psychiatrist Dr. Karl Menninger[28] contended that modern children desperately pursue "artificial belongings" because this need is not fulfilled by families, schools, and neighborhoods. For many troubled children, belonging will be found only in relationships with adults who recognize, in the words of Menninger, that "living with and loving other human beings who return that love is the most strengthening and salubrious emotional experience in the world."

# The Spirit of Mastery

Father gave me my first pony and also my first lesson in riding. The pony was a very gentle one and I was so small that he tied me in place on the pony's back. In time I sat on my horse by myself and then I rode by father's side. That was real achievement, for I was very small indeed.

—Standing Bear[35]

In addition to biological and interpersonal needs, children and adults strive for mastery of their environments. Robert White[39] referred to this need as competence motivation. Related concepts of achievement motivation and self-actualization are prominent in psychological literature. When the child's need to be competent is satisfied, motivation for further achievement is enhanced; deprived of opportunities for success, young people express their frustration through troubled behavior or by retreating in helplessness and inferiority.

The goal of Native education was to develop cognitive, physical, social, and spiritual competence. One of the first lessons a child learned was self-control and self-restraint in the presence of parents and other adults.[24] Children were taught that wisdom came from listening to and observing elders. Ceremonies and oral legends transmitted ideals to the younger generation. Stories were not only used to entertain, but to teach theories of behavior and ways of perceiving the world. Such lessons became more meaningful with repetition; the more one listened, the more was revealed.[1] Stories facilitated storing and remembering information and functioned as a higher-order mental process that ordered human existence.[30]

Competence was also cultivated by games and creative play that simulated adult responsibility. Dolls and puppies taught girls nurturing behaviors while boys were given miniature bows and arrows in preparation for the hunting role.[24] For older boys, team games promised rowdy excitement while fostering toughness and courage. Girls' games were less combative and fun was expressed through contests of skill or chance. Children learned to make articles of utility and adornment, and art was an integral part of everything they created.[21] The learning that came from such activities was effortless, because the motivation toward competency and group involvement provided powerful intrinsic reinforcers.

While play was encouraged, this was balanced by an emphasis on work as well.

> From the earliest years parents nourished the mastery of responsibility: I was asked to do little errands and my pride in doing them developed. Mother would say, "Son, bring in some wood." I would get what I was able to carry, and if it were but one stick, Mother would in some way show her pleasure.[35]

Older children were given responsibility caring for younger children. Deloria[10] describes a grandmother tending an infant asleep in a blanket on the ground. She had to leave, so called her own five-year-old son from his play and instructed him, "Cinks [son], stay here until I come back and take care of him. He is your little son, so do not leave him alone." Her tone was earnest, as if in conversation with an adult. "See that he is not stepped on, he is so tiny—and scare the flies for him." Some time later he was still on the job. While his eyes wistfully followed his playmates nearby, he stuck to his post. He had already learned that a father does not desert his son.

Success and mastery produced social recognition as well as inner satisfaction. Native children were taught to generously acknowledge the achievements of others, but a person who received honor must always accept this without arrogance. Someone more skilled than oneself was seen as a model, not a competitor:

> There was always one, or a few in every band, who swam the best, who shot the truest arrow, or who ran the fastest, and I at once set their accomplishment as the mark for me to attain. In spite of all this striving, there was no sense of rivalry. We never disliked the boy who did better than the others. On the contrary, we praised him. All through our society, the individual who excelled was praised and honored.[35]

The simple wisdom of Native culture was that since all need to feel competent, all must be encouraged in their competency. Striving was for attainment of a personal goal, not being superior to one's opponent. Just as one felt ownership in the success of others, one also learned to share personal achievements with others. Success became a possession of the many, not of the privileged few.

# The Spirit of Independence

We are not free. We do not make choices. Our choices are made for us.

—Clyde Warrior[38]

The evolution of North American culture has placed young people in a powerless situation, in which they have no meaningful role in society.[14] Persons without a sense of autonomy come to see themselves as pawns in a world where others control their destiny. Children who lack a sense of power over their own behavior and their environment are developmental casualties whose disorders are variously labeled as learned helplessness, absence of an internal locus of control, and lack of intrinsic motivation. Such young persons are scarred by alienation and school failure, and often seek alternate sources of power through chemicals or membership in a youth counterculture. While some children are deprived of autonomy, others are pushed toward premature independence.[13] The Native view is that autonomy must be balanced by continuing social controls: As opposed to contemporary white culture's pressure on children to become independent, assertive, and competitive at an early age, the child must first have opportunities to be dependent, learn to respect and value elders, and be taught through explanation for desired behavior.[24]

Traditional Native culture placed a high value on individual freedom. Survival outside of the camp circle depended upon making independent judgments, so training in self-management began in early childhood. Making one's decisions fostered motivation to attain a given goal and responsibility for failure or success. The person answered to self-imposed goals and not to demands imposed by others.[5] In contrast to "obedience" models of discipline, Native child rearing is strongly influenced by the principle of guidance without interference. Elders teach values and provide models, but the child is given increasing opportunities to learn to make choices without coercion.

The purpose of any external discipline is to build internal discipline. This view is grounded in a respect for the right of all persons to control their own destiny and the belief that children will respond to positive nurturance but cannot be made responsible by imposing one's own will on them. Even when it might be easier for the adult to "take over," adults will respect children enough to allow them to work things out in their own manner. This process was described by Maslow,[22] who studied how Blackfoot Indians were taught personal autonomy and responsibility:

> I can remember . . . a toddler trying to open a door to a cabin. He could not make it. This was a big, heavy door, and he was shoving and shoving. Well, Americans would get up and open the door for him. The Blackfoot Indians sat for half an hour while that baby struggled with that door, until he was able to get it open himself. He had to grunt and sweat, and then everyone praised him because he was able to do it himself.

Maslow concluded that Blackfoot Indians respect the child more than Americans did. Throughout his life, Maslow would remain a staunch advocate of this firm yet loving approach to building confident, emotionally secure youth.

Native elders believed that if children are to be taught responsibility, they must be approached with maturity and dignity. In the nineteenth century, Elijah Haines[20] observed that Indians "are fond of their children and treat them with the greatest respect and consideration. They rarely punish them in any way and no children seem happier." The main strategy of behavior control was kindly lecturing, which began as soon as the child was able to communicate. Blue Whirlwind relates: "We never struck our children for we loved them. Rather we talked to them gently, but never harshly. If they were doing something wrong, we asked them to stop."[21] Such gentleness did not imply permissiveness, as a Pegian elder explains:

> My parents really pushed and disciplined us
> as we were growing up. They were very clear
> as to what our responsibilities were and what
> they expected from us. If we failed to meet our
> responsibilities, we were thoroughly lectured on
> what we were doing wrong.[19]

Trieschman[36] once noted that talking with children is the principal way child-care workers package their efforts to help children. In this regard, the frequency with which lecturing is mentioned in early accounts is intriguing. Clearly this was not a lecture of the pedantic or preaching variety, although the adult was obviously in charge, and the youth was listening. Instead, unacceptable behavior was met with explanations of how others would be hurt or disappointed by such actions or how persons who acted in cruel or cowardly ways would not have friends.

Standing Bear[35] portrays an approach to rewards and punishments that challenges many contemporary theories of child management. Children were never offered prizes or rewards for doing something well. The achievement itself was the appropriate reward and to put anything above this was to plant unhealthy ideas in the minds of children and make them weak. Likewise, harsh punishment was seen as destructive.

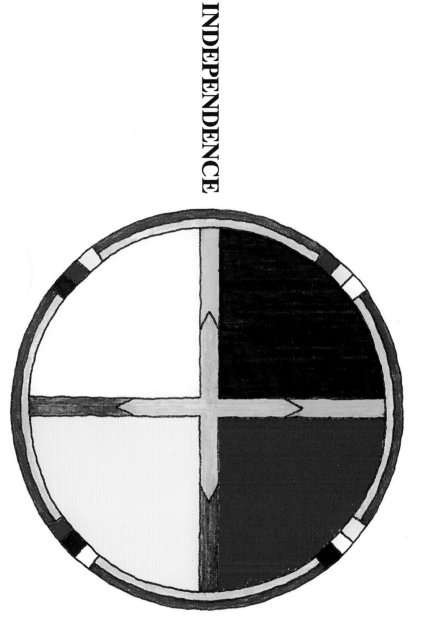

INDEPENDENCE

GENEROSITY

MASTERY

BELONGING

MASTERY

GENEROSITY

> To strike or punish a young person was an
> unthinkable brutality. Such an ugly thing as
> force with anger back of it was unknown to me,
> for it was never exhibited in my presence.

In place of rewards and punishments were modeling, group influence, discussion, and positive expectations. Standing Bear does not recall his father saying, "You have to do this," but instead he would often say something like, "Son, some day when you are a man you will do this."

The conflict between such traditional child-rearing strategies and prevailing approaches is probably strongest on the issue of autonomy for children. For example, when elders become involved in Indian schools, some professional staff may see them as "permissive" grandparents who lack a clear philosophy of discipline. In reality, the elders may be advocating a potent alternative approach that is only now beginning to be understood by contemporary behavioral experts.

In his exposition of control theory, Glasser[17] proposes innovations in child management that allow youth to exert power over their lives. His premise is that discipline never really succeeds if it does not recognize the universal need of all persons to be free, to be in control of themselves, and to be able to influence others. Hoffman[23] cites child development research showing that management by power assertion causes children to perceive moral standards as externally imposed. Often they resist such control or respond only when under the threat of external sanctions. Such studies support an alternative management strategy of "inductive discipline." This involves communicating to children the effect of their behavior on others while fostering empathy and responsibility.

Growth toward independence does not mean that a young person no longer has a need for nurturance. As Maier[25] puts it, "Children's ability to separate and manage on their own is anchored in the degree of security of their attachments." Many who work with adolescents confuse these needs by disengaging from dependency relationships while perpetuating behavioral dependence. Native child-care philosophy recognized the necessity of harmonizing apparently conflicting needs, by blending autonomy with belonging.

# The Spirit of Generosity

Grandma said when you come on something good, first thing to do is share it with whoever you can find; that way, the good spreads out where no telling it will go.

—Little Tree[6]

Children in Native cultures often sat in a circle while an older person talked to them of what was ahead as they became adults and what they should do to live good lives.[11] A recurrent message was that the highest virtue was to be generous and unselfish. Long before he could participate in the hunt, a boy would look forward to that day when he would bring home his first game and give it to persons in need.[2] Training in altruism began in earliest childhood. When a mother would share food with the needy, she would give portions to her children so they could experience the satisfaction of giving.[35]

Children were instructed to always share generously without holding back. Eastman[12] tells of his grandmother teaching him to give away what he cherished most, his puppy, so that he would become strong and courageous. Giving was a part of many ceremonies, such as a marriage or a memorial to a loved one. People engaged in gift-giving upon the least provocation; children brought food to their elder's tipis, and women made useful and artistic presents for orphans and widows. Prestige was accorded those who gave unreservedly, while those with nothing to give were pitied. To accumulate property for its own sake was disgraceful.[21]

Unlike communal societies where property was owned collectively, individual ownership prevailed in Native cultures; however, property was not acquired for conspicuous consumption but to be better able to help others. Things were less important than people, and the test of one's right values was to be able to give anything without the pulse quickening. Those not observing these customs were seen as suspicious characters whose values were based on selfishness.[10] While generosity served to redistribute wealth, giving had more than an economic rationale. Core values of sharing and community responsibility were deeply ingrained in the community.[1] Giving was not confined to property, but rather permeated all aspects of Native culture.

One does not have to live long among the Indian people today to realize that the value of generosity and sharing is still very much alive:

> A high-school boy will spend his last coins in buying a pack of cigarettes, walk into a crowded recreation room, take one cigarette for himself and pass out the rest to the eager hands around him.

> Another high-school boy will receive a new coat in the mail and wear it proudly to the next school dance. For the next three months the same coat will appear on cousins and friends at the weekly dances, and it may be several months before the original owner wears his new coat again.[5]

In this value system, one can be content without driving for status through material possessions and to measure others by intrinsic worth rather than external appearance.

Members of the dominant culture who define success in terms of personal wealth and possessions are usually unable to view positively the Native values of simplicity, generosity, and nonmaterialism. Yet, this value system has enabled an oppressed people to survive generations of great economic and personal hardships, and has made life more meaningful. Giving was the delight of the Indians: "The greatest brave was he who could part with his cherished belongings and at the same time sing songs of joy and praise."[35]

Native culture shares with Western democracy the fundamental tenet of responsibility for the welfare of all others in the community. There are many calls for a return to the spirit of service among contemporary youth to counter the attitude of "looking out for number one" that is rampant today.[8] Nearly all recent reports on the status of American education recommend more opportunities for student community service in the curriculum. Brendtro and Ness[3] demonstrate that troubled young people increase their sense of self-worth as they become committed to the positive value of caring for others. Elkind[13] suggests that helping others improves self-esteem, and increased self-esteem allows young people to "de-center" and contribute to others. Finally, the pioneer of stress psychology, Hans Selye[32] concludes that altruism is the ultimate resource for coping with life's conflicts, for in reaching out to help another, one breaks free from preoccupation with the self.

The power of caring in Native cultures is summarized in a story shared with us by Eddie Belleroe, a Cree elder from Alberta, Canada. In a conversation with his aging grandfather, he posed the question, "Grandfather, what is the purpose of life?" After a long time in thought, the old man looked up and said, "Grandson, children are the purpose of life. We were once children and someone cared for us, and now it is our time to care."

# Mending the Broken Circle

The circle is a sacred symbol of life. . . . Individual parts within the circle connect with every other; and what happens to one, or what one part does, affects all within the circle.

—Virginia Driving Hawk Sneve[34]

In *The Education of Little Tree,* a young Cherokee boy proudly declared "me and grandpa thought Indian."[6] To think in the Indian way means to look beneath the surface to see deeper relationships and explain them with clarity and simplicity. Thinking Indian also means to search for harmony among seemingly antagonistic elements, thereby avoiding the pitfall of oversimplified polarization.

Simplicity in communication is a virtue, but there is little that is simple about behavior. The same problem—for example, aggression—may stem from different causes. The same unmet need may lead to opposite behaviors—deprived of love, one child may pursue it the more while another draws away. The youth who asserts, "I don't give a damn about anybody," may really be saying, "I am unlovable." To make sense out of such paradoxes, one cannot just "observe behavior." One must learn to "decode behavior" in order to discover its meaning.

Thus far we have spoken of both courage and discouragement. Now we will "think Indian" and tie these seeming opposites together. Without belonging, mastery, independence, and generosity there can be no courage but only discouragement. DISCOURAGEMENT IS COURAGE DENIED. When the circle of courage is broken, the lives of children are no longer in harmony and balance.

Discouraged children show their conflict and despair in obvious ways, or they disguise their real feelings with acts of pseudo-courage. The effective teacher or therapist or youth worker learns to read beneath these behaviors. For example, a child's behavior may be labeled as "aggression." But to deal effectively with this angry person, one may need to answer questions like these:

- Is this revenge by a child who feels rejection?

- Is this frustration in response to failure?

- Is this rebellion to counter powerlessness?

- Is this exploitation in pursuit of selfish goals?

One cannot mend the circle of courage without understanding where it is broken. In the following listings we highlight some characteristics of children whose discouragement reflects the denial of belonging, mastery, independence, and generosity.

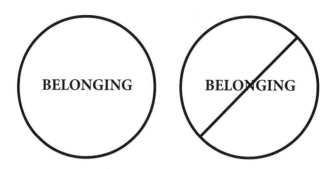

| **Normal** | **Distorted** | **Absent** |
|---|---|---|
| Attached | Gang Loyalty | Unattached |
| Loving | Craves Affection | Guarded |
| Friendly | Craves Acceptance | Rejected |
| Intimate | Promiscuous | Lonely |
| Gregarious | Clinging | Aloof |
| Cooperative | Easily Misled | Isolated |
| Trusting | Overly Dependent | Distrustful |

Some youth who feel rejected are struggling to find artificial, distorted belongings through behavior such as attention seeking or running with gangs. Others have abandoned the pursuit and are reluctant to form human attachments. In either case, their unmet needs can be addressed by corrective relationships of trust and intimacy.

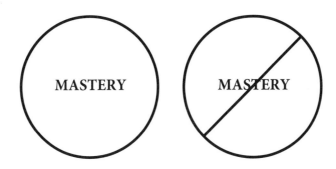

| **Normal** | **Distorted** | **Absent** |
|---|---|---|
| Achiever | Overachiever | Nonachiever |
| Successful | Arrogant | Failure Oriented |
| Creative | Risk-Seeker | Avoids Risks |
| Problem-Solver | Cheater | Fears Challenges |
| Motivated | Workaholic | Unmotivated |
| Persistent | Compulsive | Gives Up Easily |
| Competent | Delinquent Skill | Inadequate |

Frustrated in their attempts to achieve, children may seek to prove their competence in distorted ways, such as skill in delinquent activity. Others have learned to retreat from difficult challenges by giving up in futility. The remedy for these problems is involvement in an environment with abundant opportunities for meaningful achievement.

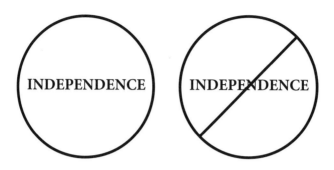

| Normal | Distorted | Absent |
|--------|-----------|--------|
| Autonomous | Dictatorial | Submissive |
| Confident | Reckless/Macho | Lacks Confidence |
| Assertive | Bullies Others | Inferiority |
| Responsible | Power Struggles | Irresponsible |
| Inner Control | Manipulative | Helplessness |
| Self-Discipline | Rebellious | Undisciplined |
| Leadership | Defies Authority | Easily Led |

Fighting against feelings of powerlessness, some youth assert themselves in rebellious and aggressive ways. Those who believe they are too weak or impotent to manage their own lives become pawns of others. These young people need opportunities to develop the skills and the confidence to assert positive leadership and self-discipline.

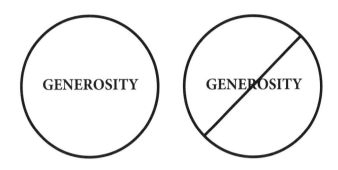

| Normal | Distorted | Absent |
|--------|-----------|--------|
| Altruistic | Noblesse Oblige | Selfishness |
| Caring | Indulgent | Affectionless |
| Sharing | Plays Martyr | Narcissistic |
| Loyal | Co-Dependent | Disloyal |
| Empathic | Overinvolved | Hardened |
| Prosocial | Servitude | Antisocial |
| Supportive | Bondage | Exploitative |

Without opportunities to give to others, young people do not develop as caring persons. Some may be involved in pseudo-altruistic helping or they may be locked in servitude to someone who uses them. Others plunge into lifestyles of hedonism and narcissism. The antidote for this malaise is to experience the joys that accrue from helping others.

When courage has been denied, people lose that sense of harmony with self and others that Karl Menninger[27] once called "the vital balance." This harmony can only be created or reclaimed in environments that embody the core values represented by the circle of courage. The child's need for belonging is nourished without neglecting the corresponding need for autonomy. The youth is taught to make independent decisions and to respect the wisdom and advice of adults. Achievement and mastery empower acts of greater service. The circle of courage is whole. The Indian spiritual leader moves his hand in the sign for "all," a horizontal circle at the level of the heart, and declares, "All things are one: the rock, the cloud, the tree, the buffalo, the man."[31]

## A Better Way

Pioneer educator and anthropologist Ella Deloria blended the best elements of Native American culture with American life. Growing up on a reservation in the 1890s, she acquired the traditions and values of her Sioux ancestors. She lived and studied in New York, earning a degree in ethnology from Columbia University, and beginning a lifelong working partnership with Franz Boaz and Margaret Meade. This urban New Yorker maintained close contact with her traditional people, recording their way of life. Interspersed with her teaching career, she published ethnological studies explaining Native wholeness and harmony in human relationships. In this example, a young murderer is brought before the victim's community to be sentenced by Sioux wisdom:

> The angry relatives debated the kind of punishment fitting the crime while the wise elder listened. After a good while he began to speak. Skillfully, he began by going along with them.

"My brothers and Cousins, my Sons and Nephews, we have been caused to weep without shame. . . . No wonder we are enraged, for our pride and honor have been grossly violated. Why shouldn't we go out, then, and give the murderer what he deserves?"

Then, after an ominous pause, he suddenly shifted. . . . "And yet, my Kinsmen, there is a better way!"

Slowly and clearly he explained the better way. It was also the hard way, but the only certain way to put out the fire in their hearts and in the murderer's.

"Each of you bring to me the thing you prize the most. These things shall be a token of our intention. We shall give them to the murderer who has hurt us, and he shall thereby become a relative in place of him who is gone. . . . And from now on, he shall be one of us, and our endless concern shall be to regard him as though he were truly our loved one come back to us."

The slayer was brought to the council not knowing what his fate was going to be . . . but the council's speaker offered him the sacred pipe saying,

"Smoke now with these your new relatives, for they have chosen to take you to themselves in place of one who is not here. It is their heart's wish that you shall become one of them; you shall go out and come in without fear. Be confident that their love and compassion which were his are now yours forever." And during that speech, tears trickled down the murderer's face. He had been trapped by loving kinship . . . and you can be sure that he made an even better relative than many who are related by blood, because he had been bought at such a price.[10]

# PART III
# The Reclaiming Environment

To be reclaimed is to be restored to value, to experience attachment, achievement, autonomy, and altruism—the four well-springs of courage.

Sociologist Martin Wolins once observed that the ideal of the "reclaiming" environment was best exemplified by the work of the Polish youth work pioneer, Janusz Korczak. Dr. Korczak was a pediatric physician who directed a school for Jewish street children in Warsaw from 1912 to 1942. The century's leading champion of youth empowerment, Korczak authored 20 books, from his earlier *How to Love a Child* to his final *Ghetto Diary,* which was written while living under Nazi occupation. He saw children as the ultimate underclass and denounced adult oppression, whether by stifling love or dictatorial domination. He believed that great untapped potentials of youth were masked by traditional education and child care:

> We fail to see the child, just as one time we were unable to see the woman, the peasant, the oppressed social strata and oppressed peoples. We have arranged things for ourselves so that children should be in our way as little as possible. . . . A child's primary and irrefutable right is the right

to voice his thoughts, to actively participate in our verdicts concerning him.[37]

Korczak believed that the child—though weak, dependent, powerless, and inexperienced—must be treated as "a citizen in embryo." He called for a deep respect for the dignity of children, education that would unleash motivation and intelligence, and the responsible involvement of youth in creating just and caring communities. Such are the foundations of the reclaiming environment.

This section outlines principles and approaches for working with children of discouragement. Four essential elements of the reclaiming environment are addressed:

1. RELATING TO THE RELUCTANT examines strategies for establishing positive relationships with youth whose lives have been marked by alienation.

2. BRAIN-FRIENDLY LEARNING presents alternative methods for organizing learning experiences to reverse patterns of failure and futility.

3. DISCIPLINE FOR RESPONSIBILITY discusses management approaches that counter irresponsibility and rebellion by mobilizing positive youth involvement.

4. THE COURAGE TO CARE presents programs for fostering prosocial values and behavior in youth whose lives are self-centered and lacking purpose.

Our discussion of these elements of the reclaiming environment will be grounded in four "profiles in development." These are attachment, achievement, autonomy, and altruism, the psychological foundations of courage. Reclaiming requires moving beyond deviance and dysfunction to address the young person's most basic unmet needs.

# Relating to the Reluctant

He drew a circle to shut me out.
Heretic, rebel, a thing to flout.
But love and I had the wit to win.
We drew a circle that took him in.

—Poet Edwin Markham
in "Outwitted"

Adults who work with youth have long been aware of the awesome power of relationships. This was a dominant theme of the early writings in education, counseling, and youth work. However, as professional literature became more scientifically oriented, relationships were increasingly ignored. Now there are signs of a renewal of interest in the synergistic power of human relationships.

Research shows that the quality of human relationships in schools and youth service programs may be more influential than the specific techniques or interventions employed. Teachers with widely divergent instructional styles can be successful if they develop a positive classroom climate. Counselors trained in different methodologies succeed or fail to a large extent based on the quality of rapport they build with clients. Behavior modification systems can work well for some adults but backfire if authority figures cannot build a tone of positive relationships.

Most of those who work with youth have a desire to build positive relationships. They know that if they are liked and respected by their charges, their days will be less frenzied and more productive. Student teachers or novice youth workers have heaved great sighs of relief when they have realized that they can "get along" with youth.

Other adults are locked in narrow professional roles that insulate them from genuine relationships with students or clients. Some keep aloof from difficult youth in the belief that "distance" is necessary to maintain "authority and respect." Others write off a certain percentage of difficult youth as destined statistical failures who will consume a disproportionate amount of time. Still other adults may wish to help but may lack the skills to relate to reluctant youth.

There are striking differences between youth who reach out to others and those who do not. Relationship-reluctant children may be fearful, suspicious, or antagonistic. They may be superficially charming but expert at keeping adults at an emotional arm's length. If they form peer attachments, these are typically with others who also distrust adults. They are likely to have parents who are low in nurturance and affection skills and may be either overly harsh or indulgent. These youth may lack social skills, including empathy, and are likely to exhibit delinquency, substance abuse, and premature sexual activity.[5]

## Profile of Attachment

> The most important observation you can make
> is when you become a glimmer in the child's
> eyes and he becomes a glimmer in yours.
>
> —Albert Trieschman

A growing body of research in psychology and sociobiology has demonstrated that attachment is a powerful universal need in humans.[7, 51] Human attachment is first seen in the bonds a child forms with primary caretakers. As with other species of mammals, the child doesn't have to "learn" to be attracted to adults, for this attraction is innate. As the youngster's social world expands, attachments are broadened to include close relationships with other significant adults and friends of the same or opposite sex. Older children can better handle being apart, but they also turn to parents in times of crisis, even into adulthood.

An early example of attachment behavior is seen in a young child who is separated from a parent in a strange situation. Normally the child shows marked distress and tries to re-establish closeness by "attachment behaviors" such as seeking physical contact. Children reared by neglectful or abusive parents learn that adults cannot be relied on to meet their needs for attachment. They are described as having "insecure attachments" because they are torn between the desire for close contact with the adult and contrary feelings of anger or anxiety.[2]

Relationship-reluctant children need corrective relationships to overcome insecure attachments. The helping adult must be able to offer warm, consistent, stable, and nonhostile attachments. Because such youth may reject friendly overtures, the adult must find ways to become more attractive to the youth while minimizing threat. This encourages relationships unencumbered by ambivalent emotions, or in the words of Hobbs, "intimacy with safety."[30]

Like Harlow's baby monkeys who kept reaching out to their abusive mothers, children with insecure attachments do not quickly give up on rejecting adults. What was formerly called "attention-seeking behavior" now appears to be better understood as "attachment behavior," namely the persistent effort to reach out and establish a secure relationship with others. Whereas adults were once instructed to "ignore" attention-seeking behavior with the goal of extinguishing it, such advice must be qualified by emerging developmental research. It seems that previous fears of spoiling children with dependence nurturance may not be justified. In fact a number of studies reveal that absence of dependence support creates greater havoc in a child's development:

> Children who oppress their caregivers with severe demands for attention are often youngsters who have suffered from too little individualized attention.[44]

Adults who unwittingly use withdrawal of affection for behavior management unwittingly give testimony to the high value most children place on the love of an adult. If the child is attracted to the adult, love-withdrawal may well establish short-term control. But for many, love is their primary unmet need. This is a central question that divides theories of psychology: whether one must behave in order to be loved, or must be loved in order to behave.[35]

The most potent behavioral influence that an adult can have in the life of a child comes when an attachment has been formed. Adults who fear that strong relationships will lessen their authority and influence with youth are misinformed. In the words of Korczak, "Your authority is based on the strength of your status as a beloved and admired model person." The existence of a positive relationship provides two very powerful teaching tools to the adult:

*Social Reinforcement.* Youth are much more responsive to encouragement or correction that comes from an adult whose opinion is valued.

*Modeling.* The most fundamental of all "discipline" techniques is when a youth becomes a "disciple" by adopting the adult's values and behavior.

Furthermore, research indicates that children who are securely attached to significant adults become more curious, self-directed, and empathic. In a very real sense, attachment fosters achievement, autonomy, and altruism.

## The Revival of Relationship Technology

There are no "10 easy steps in relationship building." George Thomas[61] suggests that our passion for cheap, "quick fixes" to the problems of youth has kept us from creating more effective systems of meeting their needs:

> In short order we have tried scaring them straight, loving them tough and seducing them with rock/jock models. We have manipulated them with reward systems like so many black boxes, warned them "no pass/no play," asked them to "just say no," and when all else has failed, introduced them to a sanctioned world of drug use aimed at preventing everything from pregnancy to paranoia. . . . In exchange for paying less and less personal attention to children's developmental needs, we are earning increasing doses of disrespectful and incompetent behavior.

Thomas concludes that if children's needs are to be kept paramount, then "relationship technology" must be revived and retooled. While one cannot provide a cookbook of techniques for human attachments, there is a solid base of information on the most effective ways of relating to the reluctant. In this section, we draw from the knowledge base of practice wisdom 10 concepts that can serve as guidelines for the "revival of relationship technology."

1. *Relationship Is an Action, Not a Feeling.* Positive, trusting relationships are the bulwark of success in work with challenging children and youth. This is not a "touchy-feely" truism but is based on a half-century of hard data from research in education, treatment, and positive youth development.[10] Students who hate teachers and schools can only be engaged by adults who can connect with such youth and excite their latent desire

for learning. Success in counseling and therapy is based less on technique than on the existence of a "helping alliance." Resilient youth who surmount unbelievable hardships are usually those who have bonded to positive adult models.

Long before science proved the power of relationships, pioneers in psychology and education discovered this on their own. Eric Fromm[19] corrected those who saw relationship as a feeling and insisted that relationships were based on actions— specific helping behaviors that created powerful change. In the first book published for teachers in the United States, G. Samuel Hall (1829) described how an adult who is able to connect with a student has an awesome potential impact on the course of that young life:

> If you succeed in gaining their love, your influ-
> ence will be greater in some respects than that
> of parents themselves. It will be in your power
> to direct them into almost any path you choose.
> . . . You have the power . . . to make them kind,
> benevolent and humane, or, by your neglect
> they may become the reverse of everything that
> is lovely, amiable and generous (p. 47).[23]

2. *Crisis Is Opportunity.* The most difficult youth are those who create trouble rather than friendships. If one were to wait for such young people to warm up to the adult, it might never happen. However, the very turbulence of their lives can work to the adult's advantage. Successful youth workers have long recognized the great hidden potential of turning crisis into opportunity. Instead of bemoaning the problems such youth create, adults must use these situations as opportunities for teaching and relationship building.

Frequently a young person who is experiencing stress will intensify attachment behavior. For example, when street-wise youth first encounter the strange and unsettling environment of a wilderness camping trip, they initially stick very close to the adult guide. At such times, the individual is more vulnerable and receptive to adult attachment.

Too often, behavioral crises elicit adult responses that widen the relationship gulf. However, when the adult manages these crises with sensitivity, the relationship bonds will become more secure. A high school teacher enrolled in a course on behavior management shared this example:

> Rob entered first period class 10 minutes after the bell, looking disheveled and agitated. I asked for his late pass and he swore and stormed from the room. I stepped into the hall to confront him about his behavior but recalled our discussion of "crisis as opportunity." I called him back and asked simply, "What's wrong, Rob?" "What's wrong!" he exclaimed. "I'm driving to school and my car gets hit. After we get through with the police, I'm late into the building and get stopped by the principal. When I tell him what happened he tells me to get to class. Now you send me out of class!" He whirled around starting down to the office. "Where are you going?" I asked. "To get a pass!" he replied. "That's OK, Rob, enough has gone wrong for one day; you're welcome in class." His hostility melted in tears. After a moment he regained his composure, thanked me and we went back in the room.

3. *Loving the Unlovable.* Very often, the child most in need of attachment is the one least likely to elicit nurturant behavior from adults. Some even try to make themselves repugnant to the adult to fend off relationships. One therapist says that when he encounters such an "unlovable" person, he tries to visualize how

the individual might have looked as a small child, thereby correcting his own negative bias. Fritz Redl[57] strongly attacked the common notion that some children are so bad that they "don't deserve" positive attention:

> The children must get plenty of love and affection whether they deserve it or not. . . . Gratifying life situations cannot be made the bargaining tools of educational or even therapeutic motivation, but must be kept tax-free as minimal parts of the youngster's diet, irrespective of the problems of deservedness.

Some children may not be "attractive" enough to those in their life to secure the nurturance they need from peers or adults. If teachers are drawn only to the brightest students, those who are undistinguished may become "the forgotten half." Children who are withdrawn or strong-willed or those with mental or physical inadequacies may not find others lining up to build relationships with them. The child who is from a different economic or cultural background is sometimes ignored or rejected. Adults need to take affirmative action to enhance the attractibility of all young persons to their peers. This will require teaching students to see the positive qualities in all persons as well as helping the reluctant youth to become a more attractive candidate for friendship.

4. *Disengaging from Conflict Cycles.* One of the most important skills youth workers can acquire is to avoid being lured into counter-aggression with difficult youngsters.[55] Such young people have not had their needs met and have acquired a negative view of self and the world. This leads to a "self-fulfilling prophecy" as the child attempts to understand and rationalize mistreatment by adults. For a child who has found adults to be physically and emotionally abusive, it makes sense to distrust them and to reject their friendly overtures. Thus, even when he

encounters helpful adults, he is likely to respond with hostility or avoidance.

Typically the adult is lured into responding in kind, thereby fulfilling the child's negative prophecy about adults. This is likely to fuel further negative interactions, thus setting in motion a self-perpetuating conflict cycle. The adult who is not aware of this process developing will inadvertently strengthen the negative behavior in the youth. An angry youth provokes adults into becoming aggressive. A depressed youth makes the adult feel like giving up. The conflict cycle becomes a type of reverse behavior modification where the adult models the maladaptive behavior of the youth. Dr. Nicholas Long[41] developed the "conflict cycle model" as a way of training teachers and youth workers to disengage from self-defeating behavior in their attempts to manage difficult youth.

5. *Earning the Trust of Youth.* Trust is an essential ingredient in building effective relationships. Ideally, children grow up with the belief that most adults can be trusted; however, many youngsters make the opposite assumption. A major hurdle in the re-education process is to help the child build a new kind of relationship with an adult who can be trusted for support, understanding, and affection.

Trust develops over a period of time in predictable stages, which we have called casing, limit-testing, and predictability.

a) *Casing.* At the initial encounter, a youth experiences much uncertainty and has a need to "check out" the adult. How the adult approaches the youth, how much power the adult wields, how others respond to this adult—all such observations are crucial data to a child who sees adults as a threat. Children usually curtail their normal behavioral responses during the casing stage, resulting in to the oft-reported honeymoon period.

b) *Limit Testing.* After the adult has been sufficiently scrutinized, the young person will need to personally try out interactions. Perhaps the child is distrustful of the adult's friendly manner. The child may purposely misbehave or provoke the adult to see if this person is really any different than all the others he has known. A calm but firm manner is needed to avoid either capitulating to the child or confirming his view that this adult is like all the rest.

c) *Predictability.* The previous two stages have provided a foundation for a more secure and predictable relationship. This may or may not be a trusting relationship, but both adult and child know what to expect from one another.

Trust is a reciprocal process. Often the adult does not trust the child any more than the child trusts the adult. One way to build trust is to extend it. Floyd Starr always looked for ways of giving youth opportunities to show they were deserving of trust. On occasion he would even ask the most untrustworthy adolescent to chauffeur his car. Of course, it would be naive and irresponsible to lay purses in front of thieves just to show that we are trusting. Trust must be extended in safe and manageable doses. The adult must be vigilant to ensure that trust is not violated, yet not appear to be "spying" on the youth, for this would only deepen mistrust. If the youth takes advantage of a trusting adult, this becomes an excellent opportunity for teaching lessons about the importance of trust.

Trying to persuade a skeptical youth that "you can trust me" is likely to heighten distrust. It may be better to simply acknowledge the distrust: "I know you don't feel you can trust me yet, and that's alright." The young person trusts when cumulative experiences prove that this adult is worth the risk. To trust is to make oneself vulnerable: to know people might hurt or betray us but to bet that they will not.

*6. Relationship Building Is an Endurance Event.* Those who seek quick and dramatic changes in a child should recognize that patterns laid down over a lifetime may be slow to change. A handicap of being a young professional is that one has not yet had the chance to see the longitudinal progression of young lives. It takes great persistence and patience to keep returning day after day to encounter a youth who seems oblivious to one's overtures. It is important to remember, as Nick Hobbs often would say, "time is our ally."

> Louise would greet me each day with a hostile or sarcastic remark. At first I tried to ignore or make light of these comments, but they troubled me a lot. With the help of a senior colleague, I learned to shed this anger and keep a positive, inviting attitude to her. After many months, she gave one of her typical "you again?" nonwelcomes and I said "maybe someday we can talk about what makes you so unhappy." To my shock she responded with "When?" That afternoon we sat on the steps of the school after classes were dismissed, and she poured out feelings of total worthlessness. Thereafter, her greetings were not always warm, but she seemed to know that I understood. I left that school before she graduated, and did not see her again for 20 years. I ran into her in the lobby of a Philadelphia hotel where we were both part of 15,000 professionals attending a conference. She proudly shared that she had finished her Ph.D. and was looking for a position on a college faculty.

*7. Conducting Therapy on the Hoof.* Fritz Redl[57] wrote about a new system of "life space" counseling which he jokingly called "therapy on the hoof." His life space interview was an alternative to the superficial "moralistic" talks that adults often have with children. Unlike formal therapy, these encounters would take place in the child's world by adults that are part of his life space. One would not wait until a scheduled counseling session, but deal with the incident when it is fresh in the child's experience.

Many youth workers are intimidated by entering into serious discussions with difficult youth because they do not have formal training in some system of psychotherapy. While skillful counselors can make important contributions, it would be well to debunk the myth and mystique surrounding psychotherapy. Sometimes an adult who is actively involved in the life experiences with a youth can engage in more genuine and helpful communications than can a therapist tethered to an office desk. This is seen in this "letter to counselors" written by a mother of a suicide victim:

> I wish you could hear the tape that David made on the night he died. He said on the tape that he had trusted you to help him. He was angry that you didn't help him, that you simply repeated back to him what he had just said. Adolescents are smart. They don't want nondirective listening when they need concrete help. Once David discovered that you were just parroting his statements, he gave you the answers you were looking for. He also gave up on finding help.[67]

Redl proposes using problems and crises as teaching opportunities. This is a clear alternative to either overly directive, moralistic preaching or totally nondirective counseling. Nicholas Long refined this frontline counseling strategy, which he calls Life Space Crisis Intervention (LSCI). This is a straightforward, practical approach to problem solving that can be used by teachers, youth workers, counselors, and others who work with challenging youth. This is a brief summary of the process[9]:

*Select an Incident.* The LSCI should be reserved for situations that lend themselves to discussion. For example, one such situation could involve a youth who has announced that he hates a certain teacher and is going to quit school.

*Gain the Child's Perception.* The initial goal is to discover how the child views the situation. For example, the youth seems to believe that a certain teacher "always picks on me" and "hates my guts." The adult encourages the expression of the youth's view, however distorted and inaccurate, while not necessarily agreeing. This non-adversarial communication lowers the defenses of the youth.

*Clarify Distortions.* As the youth becomes more trusting, it will be possible to consider alternative views. The adult now helps to clarify distortions in the youngster's perceptions. For example, the adult may review the sequence of events that triggered the disagreement between the teacher and youth and help the youth see how the incident appeared from the teacher's point of view.

*Develop a Plan of Action.* Once the problem is clarified, the adult and youth can together examine alternative solutions. It is important that the youth feel ownership of the final plan of action. For example, it might be decided that a conference with the teacher be used to develop a more amicable working relationship.

William Morse cautioned against viewing the life space interview only as a set of counseling techniques, for it is a prototype of how one can relate effectively with other persons. One must be receptive to their point of view, present alternative views in a nonmoralistic manner, and support them as they make decisions that will affect their lives.

8. *Respect Begets Respect.* Obedience can be demanded from a weaker individual, but one can never compel respect. In most children's programs, it doesn't take long to see that adults expect to be treated with more respect than they demonstrate. Adults confiscate harmless personal property, push students into lines, and ignore urgent requests for bathroom breaks. Sometimes they intentionally embarrass students with questions. Principals may grab kids by the shirt and toss them against lockers. These adults command obedience but they own very little respect.

> Helen, a teacher aide in a middle school, had difficulties building positive relationships with the students she supervised. She ruled her small domain like a petty tyrant. For example, a student who asked to borrow a pencil had to remove a shoe and leave it with Helen as a "deposit." On the playground she vigorously enforced the "keep your jackets zipped" rule on chilly days by forcing violators to stand along side the building with their jackets unzipped.

Most disrespectful behavior is more subtle. Adults may actually believe they are acting in the best interests of the child, but there is a quality of paternalism that borders on oppression. Human service professionals have a long history of patronizing, infantilizing, or dehumanizing the very persons they are pledged to serve. While they may be unaware of their basic disrespect, young persons are not.

9. *Teaching Joy.* Nicholas Hobbs, who founded the Re-ed schools for troubled children, put forth the principle that each child should know some joy each day and look forward to some joyous event for the morrow. A past president of the American Psychological Association, Hobbs indicted his own profession for its one-sided literature on anxiety and guilt and its almost total ignorance of how to develop joy in people's lives. The

teacher-counselors in the Re-ed schools see their job as helping bring the simple joys of life into the educational experience of young people. Joy should be reciprocal; only staff who truly share joy with children can teach joy.

> At camp one summer, a teacher-counselor devised a game called "Peanuts." Early each morning, every member of the Bobcats group received a small piece of brown cardboard, cut in the shape of a peanut. On the peanut was written the name of some person at camp: the cook, the director, the counselor in charge of the water program, or a child in another group. . . . During the day, the child had to do something that would make his Peanut happy, without revealing why it was being done. Everything had to be kept secret—the names of the Peanut, what was done, and so on. Then each night, before going to bed, the group would meet and each child would reveal the name of his Peanut for the day and what he had done to make them happy. . . .While the game was going on, excitement ran high, the group was very closely knit, conduct was excellent, and everyone had a good time. It was all but impossible for a Bobcat to behave disturbed that week. A similar game has been worked out for older groups. It is called "Secret Agent" or "Hit Man."[30]

10. *The Invitation to Belong.* With the advent of mandatory education, public schools were able to coerce rather than invite the attendance of students. Except for children of the wealthy, students who did not feel they belonged had no other options but to endure until they could become dropouts or dumpouts. But the doctrine of educational "choice" has challenged this state

of affairs. The growth of alternative education, open enrollment, and reasonably priced private schools has permitted many young people to decide where they might best belong. It is not surprising that this is unsettling to some educators, because now it is not just schools who can reject children, but children who are empowered to reject schools.

The traditional school is far less hospitable to its consumers than the friendly fast-food restaurant. It is not uncommon to be greeted by a terse sign requiring one to check in with the office. There one waits in a dismal excuse for a lounge, perhaps accompanied by students who have been sent from class. A plastic voice on a public address system blares out trivial announcements: a contrived congratulation to the winning volleyball team is balanced by a list of those students who are required to be incarcerated after school for detention. There is no question that one is an "outsider" on someone else's turf.

In contrast to the unfriendly school, other schools are creatively organized to foster a sense of belonging. An example of an inviting climate is that offered by a nationally recognized exemplary school, O'Gorman High School in Sioux Falls, South Dakota. This parochial high school attracts 700 students, including many who are not allied with the sponsoring denomination. The major draw is the caring community that has been created by principal Dr. Tom Lorang and his co-workers:

- Freshman students are invited to a two-day "unity weekend" over the Labor Day holiday. They are welcomed as they enter the parking lot by some of 90 senior volunteers who help carry sleeping bags and luggage into the school. The seniors have themselves participated in an earlier weekend retreat where they received training in peer helping and leadership skills. They then assume responsibility for providing positive leadership to the newest members of their community. After two exciting days, freshmen have forged a strong *esprit de corps* with peers, faculty, and older students.

- Transfer students from outlying communities who have no preexisting peer relationships at this school receive a special invitation to a picnic and water-slide party hosted by a school counselor and the natural peer helper organization. These students who would have entered without knowing any other students are now tied to a subgroup of youth from similar situations.

- The school year begins with a gala picnic and football game organized by alumni, parents, and supporters. Colorful hot-air balloons ascend from the field and parachutists drop in with the game ball. Ten thousand spectators have paid admission for this fund-raiser to celebrate the beginning of another year.

- A strong advising system anchors each student in a close relationship with a small cadre of peers and a teacher-counselor. School staff try to build a sense of relationship to all students, even those they do not have in class. Each month there is a school-wide convocation where every staff member, from cook to principal, joins with students in a shared community observance.

Every young person has a deep need to belong. Children with the greatest unmet needs for relationship are often those most alienated from adults and peers. Schools and youth work programs must make a planned and concerted effort to nourish inviting relationships in a culture of belonging. The challenge with these young people, in the metaphor of poet Edwin Markham, is to draw a circle to take them in.

## Synergistic Relationships

Positive individual relationships between adults and youth are the foundation of successful programs of education, group care, and treatment. However, these are what researchers call "necessary but not sufficient conditions." That is to say that positive individual relationships must be present in combination with other variables for the desired effect to be achieved. Four other kinds of relationships are also crucial to the development of the reclaiming environment.

*Peer-Group Relationships.* Years ago, psychologist Fritz Redl lamented his frustration of trying to reach a youngster when "the gang was under the couch." Too often staff who are expert at building individual relationships are less effective at fostering positive peer-group relationships. Those who fail to develop effective ways of dealing with the power of youth subcultures risk the destruction of their efforts. Whatever relationships or reinforcers adults may employ often seem puny competitors with the persuasive power of peers. There is now abundant evidence that successful programs for youth are those that foster the development of positive, cooperative group cultures by meaningful youth involvement.

*Staff Teamwork Relationships.* Nothing can be more unsettling than a cohesive group of difficult youth confronting a disjointed, chaotic staff. Thus, another necessary but not sufficient condition for the powerful environment is solid staff teamwork. In spite of much rhetoric about the importance of teamwork, it is seldom the highest management priority, and few schools or youth agencies ever achieve anything remotely resembling teamwork. Locked in departmental territories, loaded down by layers of middle management, staff "do their own thing" oblivious of the impact on program effectiveness. Howard Garner[20] pulls few punches in describing the "organizational bedlam" that characterizes education and human services. This problem can be addressed by employing effective models of collaboration and by working toward an interdisciplinary perspective in staff development.

*Teamwork Relationships with Parents.* Here again, our rhetoric is not matched by performance. Staff who exert much energy in working with children are seldom as enthusiastic about working with parents. Professionals who see parents as "the problem" and themselves as "rescuers" cannot effectively gain the trust of parents. It is easy to stereotype parents as unmotivated, inadequate, and even mentally ill. All too readily, we adopt the half-truth or fiction that parents are not "workable," thus leading to a self-fulfilling prophecy where we write off the family without really trying. Research suggests that successful programs involve parents as partners with professionals. But unequal partnerships are seldom effective; this means that staff must approach parents with some goal other than controlling them or treating them as patients in need of treatment.

*Leadership Relationships.* If front-line staff are to operate as full professionals and build a climate of teamwork, then the older hierarchical and authoritarian styles will be mismatched to the task. Decisions that can best be made by staff should not be passed down from on high. Procedures and rules should offer guidance but should not hamstring professional judgment. Administrators should see their role as co-workers seeking to support their staff, not as superiors trying to dominate them. In the final analysis, only adults who are themselves empowered will be free to empower young people.

When these four constellations of relationships are in harmony, a powerful synergy is released. Youth, staff, parents, and administration bind together in mutual commitment to shared goals. This is not just an idealistic vision, but must become the measure of quality control.

If these relationships are really that important, they should be systematically evaluated. We now have available a technology for assessing the interpersonal climates of schools and youth agencies. For example, at the Starr Commonwealth Schools, staff participated in the pilot development of questionnaires that would gather data on the quality of relationships. Research and evaluation staff periodically administer these to all staff, students, and parents associated with the school on a regular basis.[47] Youth evaluate their relationships with their staff team and with their peers. Staff evaluate relationships with their peers and with their supervisors. Parents evaluate the school from the vantage point of consumers. Results are shared with staff so that they might use this information to help maintain the positive interpersonal climate of the reclaiming environment.

# Brain-Friendly Learning

Tis the custom of schoolmasters to be eternally thundering in their pupils' ears, as though they were pouring into a funnel, while the business of pupils is only to repeat what others have said before.

—Michel De Montaigne,
*On the Education of Children*
(1580)

Even within the first month of life, it is apparent that humans attempt to master their environments. Arms reach, fingers grasp, and legs kick in search of meaning. Later, before stepping into a classroom, most children continue the innate search by learning the intricacies of language and playing with passion complicated games. There is little indication of a limited "attention span" as they climb trees and play with friends. Years pass and skyscrapers, rockets, paintings, and cathedrals speak of the mind's continuing quest.

The human brain is the magnificent learning organ that makes the quest possible. But something tragic often happens to the minds of many children who are eager to achieve—oftentimes in schools where the quest is supposed to be nourished and expanded. As practiced, schooling is a poor facilitator of learning. What often passes for education is noise that interrupts the natural flow of learning. Schooling too often fragments learning into subject area, substitutes control for the natural desire to learn, co-ops naturally active children for hours in assembly-line classroom structures, and ignores both individual and cultural differences. It destroys opportunities for learning from elders, from each other, and from the new generations.[50]

## Profile of Achievement

> To do well in spelling or arithmetic, especially for students who expect and dread failure, is to know a sharp delight. It is like spitting from the top of a windmill.
>
> —Nicholas Hobbs

The desire to master is seen in all cultures from childhood onward. People explore, acquire language, construct things, and attempt to cope with their environments. It is a mark of humanness that children and adults alike desire to do such things well and in so doing, gain the joy of achievement.

Harvard clinical psychologist Robert White[64] first employed the term "competence motivation" to refer to the tendency of humans to strive to master their environment. The child who succeeds gains a strong feeling of pleasure, which fuels future motivation. Repeated failure has the opposite effect. The child learns to feel anxious in mastery situations and thus the natural desire to achieve is curtailed.

The motivation to be competent permeates all experiences of the child. Children strive for physical and academic competence. At the interpersonal level, they acquire skills for relating to others. Finally, at the personal level, each child struggles to master inner feelings and emotions.[65]

David McClelland, respected for his pioneering work in achievement psychology,[46] summarized research on practices that encourage or discourage achievement motivation:

*Adult Domination.* When adults prescribe what a youth is to do and how it is to be done, the child may remain dependent and does not learn to set and pursue personal goals.

*Obedience.* Adults who stress obedience and conformity in order to develop polite and manageable children inadvertently lower achievement motivation.

*Affection.* Adult expressions of genuine interest, pleasure, and affection can increase measured achievement.

*Expectations.* Low expectations and over-indulgence both lower achievement, while realistic challenges with a high ratio of success to failure raises motivation.

*Independence.* Autonomy must be planfully nourished from early childhood, but aloof adults who "push the child from the nest" too early do not foster achievement.

Children are caught in a tension between the desire for mastery and the fear of failure. Experience teaches a person to expect success or failure in particular situations. Some exert considerable effort, even on boring or difficult tasks, to gain the pleasure and pride of accomplishment. But for others, the fear of failure is stronger than the motivation to achieve. Youth who have learned to expect failure seek to escape further shame and embarrassment by working very hard at avoiding work. They challenge adults, endure punishment, and even go AWOL from home or school, having learned that failure is never as bitter if one does not try.

While children need a preponderance of success, they can also learn useful lessons from failure. Glasser's call for schools without failure met a skeptical audience. Failure can provide a base of information and motivation upon which to construct future success.[21] While Glasser's central point of children needing success was accurate, we also need to teach children to fail courageously. The competent child will expect success, but learn to surmount adversity. This is the core of resilience. Hemingway once wrote, "The world breaks everyone and afterward many are strong at the broken places."

Most established educational approaches were developed centuries before there was any scientific understanding of the organ responsible for learning–the human brain. Now, for the first time in history, we may be able to design education to be "brain-friendly." In the following section, we examine alternatives to the failure-oriented, brain-antagonistic structures of traditional schooling. Drawing on the work of Leslie Hart,[26] who has synthesized brain research and its implication for educational achievement, we highlight four foundations of brain-friendly learning.

## Brain-Friendly Learning Is Pattern-Making

Just how the brain works is still under debate. Viewed as an information-processing organ, the brain operates like a very complicated and highly sophisticated computer that is programmed to detect and make patterns. The brain builds programs by extracting meaningful patterns out of what it first experiences as confusion.

This pattern-making ability can best be seen in language learning. A newborn is immersed in a world of words that initially have no meaning. But in a relatively short time, without any formal instruction, the child's brain detects sound, meaning, syntax, and semantic patterns in those words. For example, a small child discovers that words ending in "s" are plural. The child successfully uses this pattern until encountering words like sheep, mouse, and deer. Remarkably, this child's brain modifies the old pattern to incorporate new understanding. By six years of age, most children have mastered a syntax and developed a personal dictionary of approximately 8,000 words.[25]

Once patterns are detected, the brain uses them to build programs. All programs consist of a fixed sequence for accomplishing some objective. The more correct the program, the greater the chance the objective will be met. If any part of the program is incorrect, it will remain so until changed. Thus, Hart sees learning as acquiring new and modifying existing programs.[26]

Traditional educational practice presumes that learning requires carefully planned, logical step-by-step lessons delivered to children in obedient and orderly environments. The notion is that the child's brain is passive, unable to organize, and must therefore be directed, organized, controlled, motivated, and managed in order for learning to occur. The presumption is that the child's brain learns best through texts and verbal instruction, while interaction with peers will only lead to chaos. Such schools are organized to make teaching easy; they are not brain-friendly for the learner.

Perhaps the group of students that suffer the most from lock-step schooling are those labeled as learning disabled. Gerald Coles[11] argues in his book *The Learning Mystique* that the majority of so-called LD students are not that way because of any brain abnormality, but rather because they have entirely normal variations in the way their brains approach learning. Parents or teachers who do not understand these differences can set up inter- actions that produce achievement problems, low self-esteem, lack of motivation, and feelings of personal powerlessness.

## Brain-Friendly Learning Is Nonthreatening

When the brain perceives threat, whether covert or overt, the brain "downshifts."[26] At such times, the older, more primitive parts of the brain that deal with emotions and reflexive "fight, flight, or freeze" behaviors are in control. When this happens, the opportunity for pattern-making in the higher-thinking brain—the cerebrum—is severely limited. The fact that the brain downshifts under threat has tremendous implications for those teaching or communicating with youth.

Threat abounds in traditional education. It emanates from teachers, other students, testing, curriculum, and the structure of the school itself. Some teachers take pride in their ability to threaten and intimidate students.

> On my first day on the job, I was told by a veteran teacher that I could do myself a real favor by putting the "fear of God" into my sixth-grade students. He proceeded to explain just how I could do that. Before the students arrived, I should place the wastepaper basket right in the middle of the doorway. After the students found their seats, I should make a grand entrance by asking in a thundering voice, "Who in the hell put the wastepaper basket in the middle of the room?" If it had been moved, he said I should simply rephrase the question, "Who in the hell moved my wastepaper basket?" No matter the location of the basket, the veteran teacher explained that the basket should be sent crashing across the room with a hard kick.

Testing and the subsequent grading can be a form of threat that can turn the most capable and courageous into uncertain and discouraged individuals. Jo Dee, a former second-grade student, is a case in point:

> Jo Dee loved horses. She found out that I liked to ride and invited me out to her parents' farm to ride quarter horses. I wasn't an expert in the saddle but I thought I could keep up with an eight-year-old. I was wrong. Jo Dee led the way

over treacherous hills and through water and trees. I was glad to get back to the farm yard in one piece. The next day, I was in the middle of reading the directions of a standardized test to my second-grade students. I heard a cry of despair and looked up to see Jo Dee making her way toward me. She clamped on to my right leg. "Please don't make me take this! I can't do this!" I was struck how paper and pencil had rendered helpless the same little girl who controlled a thousand-pound horse the day before.

Tests not only debilitate second-grade students. Albert Einstein wrote: "One had to cram all this stuff into one's mind for the examinations, whether one liked it or not. This coercion had such a deterring effect on me that after I passed the final examination, I found the consideration of any scientific problems distasteful for a year."[29]

Threats may also stem from imposing irrelevant, outdated, and uninteresting curriculum and textbooks. The brain often acts in naturally courageous ways, challenging and refusing to accept that which it determines to be useless or pointless.[43] Metric conversions, bone naming, capital memorizing, identifying and circling nouns, and listing Brazilian exports may be important to some adults but may have little relevance or consequence to the lives of students.

The recent proliferation of children labeled as having "attention deficit disorders" might better be conceptualized as an "interest deficit disorder" in the curriculum. Most of these so-called ADHD children are very actively attending, but to something the brain finds more novel, worthwhile, and adventuresome than cautious curriculum and textbook trivia.

While learning is facilitated by organized classrooms, the structure teachers use to establish control can interfere with the brain's ability to think. For many, sitting in required places for required times is a flagrant denial of the high activity level characteristic of youth. Korczak put it this way: "A child is someone who needs to move, . . . to forbid this is to strangle him, put a gag in his mouth, crush his will, burn his strength, leaving only the smell of smoke."[37]

While threats discourage learning, positive environments foster learning by freeing the higher brain. But nurturing students is seen as unnecessary affective fluff by some educators. For example, an officer of the National Association of Elementary School Principals was quoted as saying, "Middle school administrators have got their hands full just trying to educate kids, let alone creating warm, caring environments."[28] But research shows that education cannot be separated from nurturance, that we will have "affective education or none at all."[13] Pestalozzi recognized this two centuries ago when he declared, "Without love, neither the physical nor the intellectual powers of the child will develop naturally."[53]

## Brain-Friendly Learning Is Experiential

The active, experiencing child is a learning child. Janusz Korczak once suggested that teacher-training colleges should use short films of children doing such things as fishing and dragging planks with contrasting scenes of the same children in the classroom working on arithmetic problems: "He is happy when carrying bricks, dragging logs, digging a ditch, swinging an axe. If you tell him to write, memorize poetry, he changes from cheerful and exemplary to disobedient, quarrelsome, spiteful and lying."[37]

Perhaps the best current examples of brain-friendly learning emanate from experience-based philosophies. Though called by many names—experiential education, alternative education, adventure education, distributive learning, community-based education, career education—all have philosophical foundations that affirm learning is best achieved when it is active, interesting, relevant, and challenging.

Foxfire, an experiential high school program in the mountains of Georgia, is a case in point. The curriculum, teaching, and school structure are molded to fit the students, not the other way around. A primary objective of the program is to help students become capable communicators. Students are encouraged to interview community members, design and build cabins, and participate in a wealth of field experiences. The Foxfire book is designed and written by the students. Such a youth-centered program requires teachers who see beyond the grade book and canned curriculum.[66]

A notable example of brain-friendly environments is adventure education pioneered by Campbell Loughmiller.[42] The Eckerd Wilderness Educational System operates a network of such programs across the eastern United States. Although totally abandoning the traditional classroom setting, they are able to make formidable academic and social gains with previously nonachieving youth.

## Brain-Friendly Learning Is Social

Throughout the history of the human race, almost all worthwhile learning has taken place in a social setting. The human brain has developed so that it functions better in social interaction than in isolation. Frank Smith[60] has made this fact the centerpiece of the curriculum as he invites youth to become part of a "learners club." Once invited, trusted to learn, made to feel secure and part of the club, children will learn naturally. As in all healthy and worthwhile clubs, the learners club genuinely admits and accepts the novice learner no matter the skill level. Learners clubs eliminate threatening tests and other pointless ritualistic activities. Members of a learners club demonstrate attributes and behaviors that others want to emulate. A quality club provides leaders who are interested in what they are doing and in working with the novice learners.

Cooperative learning is brain-friendly learning where students work with one another to reach a mutual goal. Cooperative learning is not having students simply sit by each other in small groups, nor is it having the "smart" students do the work for the "dumb" students. Cooperative learning is not free-for-all learning. Students, in heterogeneous groups, are assigned responsibilities and tasks. They are made accountable for their participation.[59]

The benefits of cooperative learning in contrast to competition or individual learning are well documented. Research suggests that students' attitudes toward teachers and peers will become more positive, student self-esteem will increase, and students will develop higher levels of prosocial abilities (i.e., empathy and altruism) and social skills (i.e., communication, conflict management, sharing). Studies report, too, that achievement levels of students increase when they participate in cooperative learning. There are even indications that achievement on computer-assisted learning tasks will be maximized when the instruction is structured cooperatively.[34]

Why many educators fail to capitalize on the benefits of cooperative learning is puzzling. Many teachers teach the way they were taught, and seldom did this include students learning from students. They simply do not know what cooperative learning is. Others do not see learning as an inherently social activity. They cling to exaggerated myths of individualism or competition, believing one succeeds without the help of others or at the expense of others. Still others may shy away from cooperative learning because of the misconception that it takes too much time to implement.

From the beginning of human community, the brain has made use of conversation and oral stories as primary programs of verbal learning. Since life itself takes the shape of a narrative, it makes sense that the brain would specialize in that form. Around a campfire or the kitchen table, stories stoke fires that seem to burn forever in the child's brain. But most adults ignore this fact or find it difficult to elicit real conversations with youth. In direct contrast to conversation and discussion, lecture and recitation have become the primary currency of exchange in schools.

Recitation happens when the adult asks a question, usually closed ended, and pauses for an instant, scarcely giving children time to think. Any response is likely to receive truncated reinforcement, like "OK" or "uh-huh." Adults speak in questions and students speak in short, "just-enough" answers, addressed to the adult only. The questions posed by adults often put students on the spot or force them to guess the answer already hidden in the adult's brain. Such recitation is not discussion, it is not socratic questioning, and it certainly is not brain-friendly.

Recently there has been an effort to promote critical thinking skills for youth. The concern is that youth are not learning the kinds of thinking skills that will make them productive, thoughtful, and contributing members of society.

Certainly skills could be taught that would enhance the pattern-forming ability of the brain. Gifted education employs problem solving, creativity, and field research in the hopes that such exposure will make children "better thinkers." But the brain-friendly paths blazed by gifted education should be opened to traffic by all.

In one sense, this newly aroused mission of teaching the brain to think is as presumptuous as teaching the heart to pump fluid or the lungs to exchange gasses. Some advocates of teaching thinking skills overlook the simple fact that the brain is a natural learning organ that was thinking eons before schools were created. One has only to watch children at play to see the dynamic brain at work.

> In the company of family and friends, Catie celebrated her third birthday. Before the candles on the birthday cake were lit, everyone told their story. The father and mother talked about the rush to the hospital, the hurried delivery, the substitute attending doctor. The mother talked about the wonderful smells and feelings of the newborn. The father told his story about buying his daughter a coming home dress—blue with ruffles. Grandma told about her day as the babysitter for the older brother. Grandpa talked about the good weather in December that kept the roads open for the trip to the hospital.
>
> All the while the little girl listened. Unthreatened, bathed in love, her mind soaked in all that made sense to her. Her story was being told.

# Discipline for Responsibility

Obedience is demanded to achieve a person with discipline. But this is a discipline that comes from the outside and works only when one is afraid of someone who is stronger than oneself. We do need discipline, an inner discipline to order our life. What is inner discipline? To my thinking it is the opposite of blind obedience. It is the development of a sense of values.

—Gisela Konopka[36]

In spite of abundant lip-service to the notion that children should be self-disciplined, such rhetoric is seldom reflected in approaches to education and child rearing. This is not because adults conspire to keep children dependent and irresponsible. Rather, they believe that without extrinsic controls and motivation, children will behave in immature and destructive ways. This concern is well-founded, for there is abundant evidence in contemporary society that undisciplined youth are capable of creating mayhem in their own lives and those of others.

Our conference in an established hotel was rudely jolted by the Saturday arrival of six busloads of unchaperoned youth, ages 17–21. The bus company had organized this trip for a day of tubing down a river and the city's folk festival. Arriving early after an all-night trip, the hotel was not ready for them until 1:00 check-in time. While many found a quiet corner and slept, the undisciplined proceeded to trash the place. The life-buoys in the pool were broken; wrappers, beer cans, and cigarette packages were strewn about. An inebriated girl in the elevator fell over the stroller of a baby, while another waved her lit cigarette close to the head of another child. Two young men, in shorts only, wrestled in the lobby. Their peers cheered them on with obscenities while a number of children, including my own, looked on in startled disbelief.

After three years as a principal, I was accustomed to students "responding to my requests." Since nobody seemed to be doing anything, I approached them and asked them to "cut the swearing." To my authoritarian surprise, one responded, "Hey, Jim, this f... old man wants us to quit talking shit." I remember standing helpless, embarrassed, unable to resort to a paddle, a detention slip, or a policy statement. I found the manager "hiding" in his office and asked what they were going to do about this; he responded, "Well, we have to expect this; they are just being kids."

## Profile of Autonomy

> If what we are doing for children is so good for them, why do they fight us so much?
>
> —Roderick Durkin[17]

With growth and development, children show a strong need to be independent and free. Children respond in different ways when their autonomy is blocked. In the face of excessive authority, some become compliant while others feel unfairly treated and strongly resist control. In either case, children are less likely to internalize adult values if they see them as externally imposed. By providing children opportunities to exercise influence over their own lives, adults encourage the development of self-discipline.

Cross-cultural research shows significant differences in training for independence. Many American families are authoritarian; that is, parental control allows little room for the views of children. By comparison, Danish families are typically more democratic; while parental standards are upheld, children have greater input in decision making. Democratic child rearing produces children who behave in more responsible ways; these adolescents express greater feelings of autonomy and are less problematic for parents.[39] Youth transition to young adulthood without wild displays of emancipation.

The desire to acquire greater independence accelerates rapidly during early adolescence. One survey asked students to rate the importance of 24 value statements, one of which was "to make my own decisions." This value increased more between fifth and ninth grades than any other. However, although the need for autonomy increased dramatically with age, opportunities for autonomy did not. This desire for more freedom than adults are willing to give provides an essential ingredient for cross-generation conflict.[5] Adults strive for control, battling youth who strive for autonomy.

Research at the University of Michigan sought to determine the impact of autonomy on the effectiveness of treatment programs for troubled youth. Autonomy was measured with questions such as "the staff give students responsibility" and "staff order the students around." When young people saw themselves as more autonomous, they were also more supportive of program goals. They had less fear for their safety, and the overall climate was more orderly and humane.[49]

The German youth work pioneer Otto Zirker once observed that when surrounded by walls, young people make wall-climbing a sport. Youth deprived of a sense of autonomy are more likely to form negative countercultures. Adult control becomes self-perpetuating: the more one controls, the more one needs to control. Adults who struggle to manage surface behavior believe they are creating an organized environment. The reality is often an underground youth culture marked by chaos and disorganization.[63]

Psychologists have spent more years studying maladjustment in children and youth than how to create autonomous, independent, and resilient children. In the face of what seemed to be overwhelmingly difficult environments, some young people cope successfully. They are able to surmount family problems, disadvantaged neighborhoods, and inadequate schools. Research has identified a number of specific skills that underlie resilient behavior[6, 48] A resilient youth:

- builds bonds with adults and peers based on care and mutual concern

- thinks for him- or herself and can solve problems creatively

- can tolerate frustration and manage emotions

- avoids making other people's problems one's own

- shows optimism and persistence in the face of failure

- resists being put down and sheds negative labels

- has a sense of humor and can "forgive and forget"

A theme that runs through many of these skills is the attainment of a sense of autonomy, an internal locus of control where youth believe they are able to manage their lives and influence their environment. Children who acquire these behaviors become stress-proofed against the inevitable storms of life. Skills such as these could comprise the core of educational objectives in the development of responsibility and autonomy.

The most common misunderstanding in discussions about autonomy is the notion that one is advocating complete freedom. Coopersmith[15] asserted that children need autonomy within a structure. Adults who give freedom without guidance are sending youth on a journey without a map. Adults must set clear and consistent expectations so that the young person can successfully navigate life's challenges. Adults do not become preoccupied with control, but focus their efforts on mapping out the structure and values. The youth is thus given a safe environment in which to develop independence, while adults still exert a major influence.

## The Path of Freedom with Self-Control

> Far from disheartening your pupils' youthful courage, spare nothing to lift up their soul; make them your equals in order that they may become your equals.
>
> —Jean Jacques Rousseau,
> French Philosopher and Writer

These words written more than 200 years ago seem alien and strange to many because they suggest an unnatural and irrational relationship with children. For many, equality with children seems ludicrous; children lack the adult knowledge and experience essential for controlling their own lives. Consequently, children for the most part remain dependent on and at the mercy of those who are more powerful.

Korczak saw the disempowerment of children as an insidious problem of universal oppression by adults. He had an early experience that shaped his subsequent view of adult/child relationships. At age 14, young Korczak entered a literary contest and eagerly went to see what the editor would say. The man tossed his work back at him, insulted him, and sent him out of the office. Korczak was furious. "Not that my work was unacceptable," he said, "but that he acted as one who had privilege. What was the basis of his privilege? You see, he was an adult. I was but a child." Years later he was to write that the oldest underdog in the world is a child.

A society that has emancipated itself from other old prejudices clings to the oppression of children. Korczak speculated about what would happen in a "pedocracy" or government by the children. He dreamed of international conferences in Jerusalem or New York where children from throughout the world would present plays to overflow audiences of adults who rediscover their childlike sense of justice. His most popular children's book, *King Matt the First*,[38] tells of a 12-year-old boy who becomes monarch and tries to sensitize adults to the views of the young. A crusade is organized and the children march forth under a green flag to reform the world. On a more practical level, Korczak ran his school with a system of youth government and started a national journal written by children.

As radical as these pioneers sound in their calls for child equality, they challenge us to see children in another light. If respect, dignity, and justice—the ingredients of equality—are dependent on birthdays, then the disempowerment of children will persist. As Jane Addams observed, the values of a democracy should lead us to a new path in child rearing based on the principle of freedom with self-control. The following are examples of concepts and strategies that schools and youth agencies have found useful in instilling responsible freedom.

*Discipline Replaces Punishment.* All child rearing involves some assertion of the power of adults over their young. In the purest form of "discipline," an adult provides a strong model and value guidance to the young "disciple." However, this concept has mutated so that dictionaries now define discipline with the synonym of "punishment." The joining of discipline with punishment creates a psychological oxymoron. Table 3 compares these very different concepts. Discipline is a process of teaching, not of coercion. It seeks to involve youth in learning social responsibility and self-control. Discipline is impeded by the unilateral exercise of adult authority and control.

---

## TABLE 3

### A COMPARISON OF DISCIPLINE AND PUNISHMENT

| Discipline Process | **Punishment Process** |
|---|---|
| 1. Proactive focus on preventing problems | 1. Reactive intervention after problem occurs |
| 2. Natural consequences discussed with youth | 2. Adult imposes arbitrary consequences |
| 3. Respect for social responsibilities taught | 3. Obedience to authority figures taught |
| 4. Control by inner values expected | 4. Control by external rule enforcement |
| 5. Psychological and physical punishment contra-indicated | 5. Psychological and physical punishment employed |

Adapted from *Intervention Techniques for Child/Youth Care Workers* by Mark Krueger. Washington, DC: The Child Welfare League of America, 1988.

---

Children learn best from natural consequences, not from arbitrary punishments or restrictions. While this is the centerpiece of Adlerian philosophies of discipline, Rousseau had described this process much earlier:

> Punishment as punishment must never be inflicted on children, but it should always happen to them as a natural consequence of their bad action. Thus you will not declaim against lying; you will not precisely punish them for having lied; but you will arrange it so that all the bad effects of lying—such as not being believed when one tells the truth, of being accused of the evil that one did not do although one denies it—come in league against them when they have lied.

Natural consequences are powerful when they are available, but too often they are not. If there are no natural consequences, then as Dreikurs[16] suggests, adults should at least make consequences logical. An example would be the assignment to the janitorial crew for youth who had flooded the school lavatories. Too often the availability of some ready restriction means it will be used for almost everything. For example, some schools even suspend youth for skipping school. Illogical punishments only fuel anger and bitterness in alienated youth.

Pioneering child psychiatrist Richard Jenkins[33] concluded that in spite of the potential abuses of punishment, no society can exist without some negative sanctions to define limits. But children can never be effectively socialized if the balance of interventions are more punitive than positive. If punishment is to be "occasionally and judiciously used," it is essential that it come from adults who communicate an acceptance of the child. Punishment always has a destructive effect if youth interpret it as a lasting dislike or hostility from the people on whom they are dependent for love and security.

Rules are to values as obedience is to respect. It is a truism that young people "have to learn to live by the rules." But it is even more important that they develop into young persons who possess what Fritz Redl[57] called "controls from within." Pre-occupation with rules creates a kind of oppression where even the most well-meaning adults lose sight of underlying values. It is much easier to write another procedure than to teach a young person to respect the rights of others.

Often high-level administrators send down rules which underlings are to enforce and youth are to obey. These rule books may make those in power feel secure but are likely to be ignored or outmaneuvered if they are not owned by front-line staff and youth. Research on effective alternative schools for alienated youth shows that they are able to adapt flexibly to the needs of youth rather than make every decision "by the book." Rigid procedures turn professionals into clerks and technocrats. Programs that have shifted emphasis from pursuing rule viola-tors to teaching values of mutual respect create more manage-able educational climates.[22]

While effective youth workers are not authoritarian, they should possess the ability to be the strong, central force in a group setting. They move quickly to become what has been called the "alpha individual" as they assert positive social influence over the process of the group.[68] This involves being authoritative but not authoritarian. Only adults who are secure in their own sense of personal power can exercise strong yet noncoercive influence over children. Staff who feel insignifi-cant and powerless will seek power over children as an artificial means of gaining importance.

*Demanding Greatness Instead of Obedience.*[62] Many youth work professionals assume that the choice in management philosophy is between demanding obedience or allowing youth to run wild. There is another option that is neither authoritarian nor permissive. This is to demand mature, responsible behavior. It is not acceptable for youth to run roughshod over the rights of others. Hurting behavior will be challenged and young people will be held accountable, but this is done in ways that call forth the great potential of young people. But, like adults, young people do not like to assume responsibility for failures and weaknesses. They rationalize, deny, project, or excuse—anything to avoid the uncomfortable feeling that comes with knowing one has been wrong.

The rejection of responsibility becomes a high art form with youth who see others as the cause of all their problems. But taking ownership of problems is the first step in resolving them. We do a disservice by allowing youth to dodge responsibility for their actions. A person who puts off responsibility must be countered by an adult or peer who "reverses responsibility." The following are examples of this process:

- When a teen-age girl sought to excuse her poor school attendance by telling the counselor, "Well, my parents are alcoholics so what do you expect?" the counselor reversed this by saying simply, "Well, I guess it's up to you, then."

- When a drug-abusing youth rationalized that "lots of adults use drugs of some kind, too," his peers in a counseling group retorted, "how does that give you a right to mess over yourself?"

- The youth who responds to the slightest affront with aggression and brags that "nobody messes with me" is challenged to have enough self-confidence that "nobody will be able to make you feel unimportant."

When the climate of responsibility is well-established, there will be quick recognition of cop-outs and little tolerance for them. These reversals of responsibility must be carried out with deep concern, because the goal is never to attack a person, but to communicate a belief in the young person's ability to take charge of his or her life. One youth in such an empowerment program was heard explaining the ropes to a newcomer: "They even talk to you different here. Whatever you say it's like they hold up a mirror to you and you find the answer somewhere inside of yourself."

*Making Caring Fashionable.* Exploitative, hedonistic, and rebellious behavior often brings more status in certain groups of youth than does caring. Within the youth subculture, highly destructive behavior is often glamorized with a terminology that masks the real nature of the underlying values. For example, marijuana is not referred to as "flaky brown stuff wrapped in tissue paper" but something more exotic like "Acapulco Gold." Destructive chemicals become "speed" or "angel dust." A gang rape has been called by the frivolous name "gang bang" for generations.

Antisocial youth romanticize destructive behavior, and put down those espousing positive values and behavior. Helpful, sensitive, and prosocial actions are given negative labels such as "sissy," "narc," or "brown-nose." The significance of this is profound. Every culture embodies its most basic values in its language. When hurting behavior is exalted or rationalized and helping behavior is ridiculed, then a powerful value indoctrination is underway.

Unless adults challenge this moral deception, young people will be systematically socialized toward antisocial life values and lifestyles. While we may be reluctant to become involved in asserting values, there is really no choice; silence is not neutrality. While adults can have a positive effect by the quiet, caring model they present, direct verbal intervention may also be necessary to counter the pervasive impact of negative youth subcultures. The verbal communication strategy of "relabeling" has been developed as an antidote to a subcultural language that makes caring unfashionable. If young people describe hurting or immature behavior as if it were cool or fashionable, adults will relabel the behavior. Examples of this process follow:

- The subcultural idiom for theft is "rip-off." This macho-sounding term can be relabeled "being sneaky."

- If the term "truancy" has a romantic quality, it can be relabeled as "playing hide and seek."

- The youth who bullies a younger child to "show him who is boss" is confronted for "acting immature."

Helping behavior is given such labels as strong, courageous, intelligent, or attractive. Destructive acts are more accurately relabeled as immature, incompetent, cowardly, foolish, and so forth. In no case is a negative label attached to the young person, but only to the behavior. For this approach to be effective, the adult must succeed in conveying the genuine message that "this is very irresponsible behavior for such a great young person as you."

*Tapping the Spirit of Adventure.* Many of the difficulties of youth are related to the fact that they are highly spirited and adventurous. A distinctive feature of much youthful delinquency is the celebration of prowess. Such youth are not motivated by the hum-drum routine of most schools. Their search for fun and adventure often leads to excitement and kicks through risk-seeking behavior. The frightening spectacle of youth gangs in major cities has some of this quality. Many of these young people are following the code of the warrior. As they defend their turf and honor, their aggression and toughness provides evidence of "heart" or courage.[45]

Kurt Hahn[3] thought the foremost task of education was to build the prosocial values of courage, compassion, and self-discipline. He said that adults must not impose these values on youth but should instead create powerful educational experiences that spontaneously call forth the capacity within them.

By confining youth to adult-dominated activities, we are depriving them of the benefits of the "powerful curriculum."

Wilderness adventure programs provide a prominent example of such courage-building activities. When one is struggling against the elements of nature, it is not just the adult that demands greatness, but the challenge of survival itself. Such activities provide a powerful short-term learning experience for youth who cannot be reached by traditional methods. Even the most resistant youth has no need to defy the law of natural consequences, and personal responsibility is readily mastered. This is well-portrayed in this example of a youth reflecting on his wilderness experience:

> You will push yourself, and be pushed both mentally and physically further than you ever imagined possible. . . . You will feel the power overcome you, and you will know without a doubt that you have done something that will irrevocably remain with you in your mind forever. You will feel the limitations of all the things you once thought impossible for you to do slip away from your mind and you will reach the ultimate realization that there are no limits to the things you are capable of accomplishing. That will be the supreme rush.[3]

—Tommy C., age 17

*Mobilizing the Power of Peers.* Many adults view the youth subculture in a predominantly negative light. In this way of thinking, the power of peers must be opposed or at best tolerated. One of the significant rediscoveries of recent years has been to see the youth subculture as an asset, not a liability.

Even young people who have experienced serious personal difficulties can be used in positive leadership roles. Many times such youth have unique "experience" beyond that of the trained professional. For example, several nations have formal associations of young people who are or were residents in various re-education programs. These youth associations often meet parallel to large professional youth work conferences so they can engage in mutual exchange of views. The Canadian network of youth in care has even assisted the national government in developing more sensitive legislation for youth at risk. When hearings were being held in Ottawa on child prostitution, the young people amazed authorities by their ability to mobilize youth prostitutes to provide poignant testimony about this problem. Young people in that association published a book with recommendations to government policymakers on the needs of youth in transition from foster care to independent living.[56]

There are now abundant examples of creative strategies for developing positive youth leadership in educational and youth work programs. When we described one such program in the book *Re-educating Troubled Youth*[9] some years ago, we were told by a prominent writer on youth problems that it was dangerous to give responsibility to irresponsible youth. In our view, the real danger lies in these attitudes that keep young people from assuming responsible roles in our schools and communities.

A variety of innovative peer helping, peer counseling, and youth self-government programs have been instituted in schools and youth agencies. One example is the positive peer culture program in schools in Omaha, Nebraska.[62] These programs were started in secondary schools and were extended to the upper elementary level. The program's goal is to identify natural indigenous leaders who are provided special training that will enable them to help other students and improve the school climate. These youth represent all the subgroups within the school, including some cliques not seen as positive by school staff. These diverse youth are organized into small problem-solving groups where they first learn to respect and support one another and then make available their skills to the total school population. They are particularly effective in reaching youth who do not trust the formal counseling system of the school.

These peer helping groups have filled a multitude of roles. Working closely with school counselors, they have provided support to youth dealing with family problems or the death of a parent. One group supported a terminally ill high school student during the months preceding her death. A junior high principal highlighted some of the activities in which the helping groups had provided positive leadership to the school: (1) recovering stolen property, including purses, cash, watches, and numerous shop tools; (2) effectively confronting peers who were harassing and attacking students from opposing schools during a heated basketball game; (3) eliminating vandalism as a leadership group organized a student-operated monitor system; and (4) providing support and tutorial assistance to underachieving students who were considering dropping out of school.

There is a growing body of evidence that programs of peer involvement not only neutralize anti-authority behavior, but also create positive learning climates that foster social and academic development. The benefits include enhanced self-esteem, increased internal locus of responsibility, increased prosocial values, and reversal of long-standing patterns of school failure and underachievement.[62] Young people are not just the leaders of tomorrow—they have great untapped potential for responsible leadership today.

# The Courage to Care

I am the spirit of Youth! With me, all
things are possible!

—Jane Addams, American Social
Worker and Writer

Throughout history, the most successful youth workers have been able to see beyond the problems of young people to a vision of their great potential. In the first book on "adolescence," G. Stanley Hall[24] described this stage as "a second birth, marked by a sudden rise of moral idealism, chivalry and religious enthusiasm."

Writing in 1909, Jane Addams[1] proclaimed that young people have a "wonderful and inexplicable instinct for justice" that could be harnessed to counter what she called "the most materialistic period of all history." At the end of the nineteenth century, William James[32] wrote an essay on "the moral equivalent of war." He recognized the need of young people to be committed to some cause beyond themselves and saw community service as a worthy substitute for military combat. As they contributed to the greater good of society, young people would replace "self-seeking" behavior with "self-forgetfulness" and civic discipline.

The classic account in educational history of the willingness of children to serve comes from the pen of Pestalozzi. Here he describes his conversation with his orphans at Stans upon hearing that a neighboring village had been destroyed by fire:

I gathered the children round me, and said, "Altdorf has been burnt down; perhaps, at this very moment, there are a hundred children there without home, food, or clothes; will you not ask our good Government to let twenty of them come and live with us?" I still seem to see the emotion with which they answered, "Oh, yes, yes!" "But, my children," I said, "think well of what you are asking! Even now we have scarcely money enough, and it is not at all certain that if these poor children come to us, the Government would give us any more than they do at present, so that you might have to work harder, and share your clothes with these children, and sometimes perhaps go without food. Do not say, then, that you would like them to come unless you are quite prepared for all these consequences. . . . But they were not in the least shaken in their decision, and all repeated, "Yes, yes, we are quite ready to work harder, eat less, and share our clothes, for we want them to come."[54]

## Profile of Altruism

Are we, basically, but another species in the animal kingdom, or have we a nobler self, in continuous struggle with our baser part?

—Amitia Etzioni[18]

There have been many intriguing accounts about the foundations of caring behavior. Alan Keith-Lucas[35] notes that the early Greeks called a man who did not become involved with others an "idiot," which was the early meaning of the word. Among the Roman elite, it was an obligation to establish one's nobility with displays of charity to those of lesser birth *(noblesse oblige)*. More recently, many psychological theorists suggest that latent selfishness lurks beneath seemingly selfless acts of generosity. To the sociobiologist, helping behavior may result from an instinctual drive to protect related members of one's species.

Batson[4] reviewed the long history of debate about altruism in philosophy and psychology. Most recent theories of motivation assume that all human behavior, even seemingly selfless acts, are ultimately directed toward selfish goals. But research makes a distinction between genuine altruism and two types of "pseudo-altruism" or self-centered helping behavior:

- Pseudo-altruism to gain rewards or avoid punishment. Sometimes people help others because they seek personal gain or wish to avoid shame or guilt. Examples would be joining a "service club" for the ulterior motive of making more business contacts or fulfilling a 100-hour court sentence of "community service" to avoid going to jail.

- Pseudo-altruism to reduce feelings of distress. In all higher animals, distress calls evoke strong psychophysiological responses. Even young children show distress in the presence of a cry of pain or hurt from another child. This unpleasant reaction is lessened by helping behavior or by leaving the situation if the distress is too intense.

- Genuine altruism evoked by empathy with another person. Persons with empathy can understand the perspective of another. Empathy motivates helping behavior aimed at meeting the other person's needs. Of course, it is possible that genuine altruism will also lead to some social or self-rewards. However, these are not the goal of helping, simply the incidental consequences.

Empathy is the linchpin in this concept of altruism. As used by Batson, it involves the ability to de-center and take the perspective of another. There is usually both a cognitive side to empathy (understanding what another is experiencing) as well as an affective one (feeling what another is experiencing). There are natural differences in the abilities of persons to de-center and accurately understand the viewpoint of another. Empathy can be strengthened by a conscious effort to think how it would be "to walk in the moccasins" of another person.

There is a strong connection between attachment and empathy. We understand best those we see as "like us," such as relatives, close friends, members of the same gender, and persons with a common cultural background. Empathy is also easier when the helper and helpee share similar experiences, such as the empathy one rape victim would have for another. The capacity to empathize with others can be enhanced by recognizing one's relationship to them. At the highest levels of moral development, one gains a sense of being related to all of humanity. The Roman philosopher Terence put it this way: "I am human, so nothing human is alien to me."

The distinction between pseudo-altruism and genuine altruism is crucial to building genuinely caring relationships. Psychiatrist M. Scott Peck[52] notes that this concept has been expressed by all the great religious traditions:

> If we seek to be loved—if we expect to be loved—
> this cannot be accomplished; we will be depen-
> dent and grasping, not genuinely loving. But
> when we nurture ourselves and others without a
> primary concern of finding reward, then we will
> have become lovable, and the reward of being
> loved, which we have not sought, will find us.

# A Curriculum for Caring

In recent years, we have seen a revival of interest in the planful use of "service-learning" as an antidote to the narcissism and irresponsibility of modern lifestyles. Many studies and reports on education have called for community service as a vital ingredient in the school curriculum. For example, The Carnegie Council on Adolescent Development[11] proposes these goals for youth in the twenty-first century:

> The young person will embrace many virtues such as courage, acceptance of responsibility, honesty, integrity, tolerance, appreciation of individual differences, and caring about others. The young person will demonstrate all these values through sustained service to others.

It is not enough for adults to care for children; young people must be empowered to care and contribute to the betterment of their families, friends, schools, and communities. In this final section, we examine the essential ingredients for what Bronfenbrenner called "the curriculum for caring."

Kurt Hahn was one of the earliest to advocate educational activities to teach compassion. He believed that modern youth desperately needed to contribute to a cause beyond themselves, to find some *grande passion*. He noted that there were three ways to motivate such service, namely, persuasion, compulsion, and attraction:

> You can preach at them: that is a hook without a worm; You can order them to volunteer: that is dishonest; You can call on them: you are needed, and that approach will hardly ever fail.[58]

Research from the University of Minnesota indicates that voluntary community service benefits both young people and the community. Students break free of the passive role as they are asked to share of themselves. The time is ripe for training in service:

> Young people have never been more self-cen-
> tered, more concerned with money, power, and
> status, and less concerned about helping others.
> Youth have never been more violent, out of con-
> trol, and beyond the influence of their parents
> and the community.[27]

One should not assume that the blame lies with the youth alone. They are reflecting values of societal institutions, includ-ing schools designed so that some young people achieve at the expense of others.

Research documents many positive results of volunteer service. These include increased responsibility, self-esteem, moral development, and commitment to democratic values. While these are laudable goals, many educators are skeptical, believing that such programs may interfere with the school's busy agenda of academic learning. But intellectual gains can accrue from service-learning, including:

- motivating youth who are bored with school by linking academic learning with real human needs

- increasing achievement of youth who work as volunteer peer tutors

- increasing problem-solving abilities of youth

- developing more complex patterns of thinking

The Minnesota study illustrates the features of successful service programs with reflection by students on what they have learned. These are examples of student reactions:

- "As I walked through the hallway of the elementary school on my first day of leading children in theater experiences, I realized what I had gotten myself into . . .

a challenge. But as I stepped through the door I transformed from student to person."

- "I remember my first few days at Oak Terrace (a nursing home). I was scared to touch people or the doorknobs even. And I used to wash my hands after I left there every single day! Can you believe it? Now I go and get big hugs and kisses from everyone. Get this—I even eat there!"

- "My kids have so much love, touching, caring affection toward me and one another. It is amazing how much better you feel about yourself after getting all of this loving affection. It makes me wonder where, and when, we lost all that love and affection? You never see it in high school. In what grade does all this stop? Why does it stop? Does it have to stop?"[27]

Volunteer youth service programs are specifically designed to help young people overcome the narcissism of self-absorption. As they find they can make a difference in the lives of others, they validate their own self-worth. In the following section, we share examples of such programs in action.

## Hooked on Helping

For a number of years we have been involved in developing programs that teach caring values and behavior to young people who had otherwise distinguished themselves by self-centered and antisocial behavior.[62] In a discussion entitled "Hooked on Helping," we provided examples of a number of successful service-learning projects, including the following:

- Youth from an alternative school for delinquents assisted in the Special Olympics and went on camping trips with students who were blind.

- Elementary children bought groceries for needy families using money accumulated as a result of no vandalism in their school over an extended period.

- Youngsters prepared a home for a refugee family, planting flowers and bringing toys to welcome the children.

- Teenagers chopped firewood for the disabled, visited senior citizens, and organized a clown show for a day-care center.

There is now a growing body of practice wisdom on how to organize and operate such activities in schools and youth work agencies.[14] The most successful projects are exciting and spontaneous rather than regimented or highly adult-oriented. There is usually a balance between short-term projects and those designed to meet the need for long-term commitments. Activities that involve direct people-to-people contact usually have greater learning value than more indirect service. Projects that appeal to the strength of young people (e.g., "this will be a tough job") bring greater satisfaction than those that are less challenging. It is always important to involve the young people in developing, executing, and evaluating the projects.

An exciting program of service-learning has been described by Michelle Iole and Anne Dolan of the Pathway School in Pennsylvania.[31] They developed a "service club" format with adolescents enrolled in a residential school for students with learning disabilities and socio-emotional problems. Such young people have a long history as care-recipients and are convinced that they are unworthy of respect and undeserving of praise. They see themselves as damaged goods in a world that stresses excellence. Simply stated, the service club offers opportunities for growth through helping others. The projects are as basic as shoveling snow for the elderly or as complex as planning and executing a holiday toy drive for underprivileged children.

When a service club is being initiated, both children and adults often have doubts. It is important to gain the input and choice of club members in planning activities. Youth who feel forced to perform tasks that they feel uncomfortable doing will become resistant. Sometimes what appears as initial disinterest is really the child's attempt to avoid yet another failure. After being involved in several projects, however, children discover that they have the competence and power to affect the lives of others. Children who had been accustomed to hearing "don't come around here again" can scarcely believe it when adults now invite them to return and help another time.

The service club developed by Iole and Dolan regularly visits a Philadelphia shelter for the homeless called Trevor's Place. Most visits consist of bringing casseroles the boys have made and spending time with the children who live there. The shelter is named after a boy who, upon first learning of the homeless, asked his parents to drive him to the center city of Philadelphia to deliver his extra blanket to a person living on the streets. The boys had heard the story of Trevor's generosity and were motivated to follow his example:

> On one visit, we saw a number of homeless people sitting on steam vents in the surrounding neighborhood. We felt badly that we had nothing to offer them and decided to bring along some peanut butter and jelly sandwiches on our next trip. As we packed the vans on the day of our next visit, sandwiches included, Alex asked if he could bring along an old blanket of his to offer one of the homeless people on the street. Staff agreed to his request, and upon hearing this, another of the boys ran into his room and returned with his blanket.

That same evening, as we left Trevor's we intentionally drove through the most desolate part of the city. We still had sandwiches to give, and we were searching for someone who might appreciate some food on a cold December night. As we approached a dark intersection, Tim cried out from the backseat of the van that there was a homeless person on the corner. He grabbed a sandwich and climbed out the back door, running over to where an old woman sat. She clearly had all her worldy possessions surrounding her: an old shopping cart, a wooden stool, and other items that had been scavenged from the sidewalks. As Tim nervously approached her, asking if she would like a sandwich, she displayed a toothless grin and answered yes. He handed her the sandwich and, not knowing what else to say, ran back to the van.

The others questioned him, wondering what he had said, what she had said, and whether or not he had been frightened. But Tim said very little. He just sat quietly—and smiled.[31]

## Conclusion

In the final analysis, the values of courage are demonstrated in the actions of those who emerged at many times and places in history to bring dignity to the lives of children. Sometimes these were tribal persons who nurtured the sacred fires in cultures where caring for children was the central unifying theme. Throughout much of the history of Western civilization, they were lonely prophetic voices calling for a restoration of dignity to children of discouragement.

In the nineteenth century, Europe began to reawaken to the philosophies of such youth work pioneers as Itard and Pestalozzi. Across the Atlantic, the United States was still a fledgling nation when a powerful advocate for children arose in the person of Dorothea Dix. Ignoring her own frail health and the message that women should not take the lead, she tirelessly battled the abuses of orphanages, jails, and almshouses, giving birth to the modern mental health movement. In that same period, Horace Mann championed the cause of schooling for all, and he challenged young graduates of Antioch College to be ashamed to die until they had won some great victory for humanity.

The twentieth century opened with a spirit of great optimism but was to end without fulfilling its destiny as "the century of the child." The heights and the depths of this era are portrayed by the life of Janusz Korczak of Poland, champion of the child's right to respect.[8] Dr. Korczak had a distinguished career as a writer, teacher, and director of a school and orphanage for Jewish children of the street. When the Nazis occupied Poland, they moved his orphanage to the Warsaw Ghetto. He refused offers for safe passage, choosing instead to remain with his band of 200 children.

When it became clear to Korczak that he and the children soon would be shipped away to a death camp, he prepared them for what was to come. They produced a play based on Rabindrinath Tagore's *Post Office,* the story of a dying Hindu boy. Then, on the day when the soldiers arrived to get them, they were dressed in their best and departed, marching in flanks behind the biggest boy who carried a green flag. This children's crusade proceeded to the chlorinated box cars which were bound for the gas chambers of Treblinka.

Today where that factory of death once stood, only the green of grass and trees surrounding a circle of stones remain. On the various rocks are inscribed the cities or countries from which one million people came to meet their end. The only individual name on any stone reads simply "Janusz Korczak and children."

Following Korczak's death, friends recovered the manuscript for *Ghetto Diary,* which he had hidden behind a brick wall in the attic of the children's home. In his final entries made in the summer of 1942, he wonders whether anyone will ever care about what he is writing, concluding that "maybe it will be of use to someone, sometime, in fifty years or so." And then he sums up the meaning of his life in the words, "I exist not to be loved and admired, but to love and to act."

Across centuries and cultures, the saga of our forebears has been carried to us in this time and place. Now the responsibility is ours to keep their story alive. A society marked by alienation must rediscover its heritage of enduring values. Then, as Ellen Key said at the beginning of another century, these truths will be renewed in the conviction of a new generation of human beings.

# Honoring George Blue Bird

When the first edition of this book arrived from the printer, we took two copies into the South Dakota State Penitentiary. It seemed appropriate that these be presented to George Blue Bird, the artist who created the Circle of Courage paintings in the center of this book. In his early 20s, he was involved in an alcohol-related homicide. Following his arrest, he was assigned a public defender who advised him to plead guilty to manslaughter to avoid a more severe charge. George was sentenced to life imprisonment without the possibility of parole. Barely into his manhood, George was locked away, leaving behind a preschool-age daughter and an infant son. As his children grew towards maturity, he never saw them outside of the confines of the prison visitation room.

We planned to present the first copies of our book to George Blue Bird in the prison school, which at that time was a model of progressive correctional education. George spent much time at "Penitentiary High" in those days, volunteering to teach art and Lakota culture to younger Indian inmates. The school principal had received her Master's degree from our college and eagerly arranged for our presentation. Inmate students, faculty, and correctional officers crowded into the largest room in this school behind bars. A giant tattooed photographer stood poised to capture the ceremony for the prison newspaper.

We addressed the gathered audience, explaining that this book was written to reclaim troubled kids. We were honoring

George Blue Bird for his fine art by giving him the first copies, which were fresh off the presses. As he was called forward, the inmates gave George inspired applause. They were excited that one of their number was making a real contribution to keeping troubled kids from ending up in places like this prison.

Upon receiving two copies of *Reclaiming Youth at Risk*, George immediately gave one as a gift to the prison school principal in the spirit of generosity that marks his culture and character. Then, he spoke in a humble, respectful manner.

> When I first read the manuscript, I realized that this book was about me. I grew up as a youth at risk—I was an *almost person*. I *almost* finished high school. Art was my favorite subject, but the art teacher quit, the art materials were locked away, and I dropped out of school. Later I finished my GED and worked in a Native American community center in Wisconsin. I *almost* had a career. I wanted to work with Indian youth and so I *almost* went to Morningside College in Sioux City. But I was still a youth at risk, wrecking my future with alcohol.
>
> I told the judge who sentenced me that some day my life would amount to something, and now I am more than an almost person, for this book is finished. I hope someday to publish my art in a children's book about Lakota culture.

George held aloft his copy of the green book and displayed each page of colored art he had created. Pointing to the Circle of Courage he said, "This is a medicine wheel. Tribal people use the circle to show that all of life must be in balance and that we all must be connected to one another. The four colors—black, white, red, and yellow—stand for the four directions, and also for the four races. We should all live in harmony, part of the same circle."

Turning to the drawing labeled *Belonging,* George said, "I read in the manuscript that every child needs some adult who is crazy about him, so I drew myself dancing with my little son, White Buffalo. I haven't seen him since he was two months old—he would be six years old now."

George next showed the art for *Mastery.* "Here I painted myself as a boy with my grandfather who taught me to hunt. Grandfather hung burlap sacks on a clothesline that could be moved with a pulley. He had somebody keep the sacks in motion while I tried to shoot them with my bow and arrow. Grandfather said, 'You'll probably miss most of the time, but that doesn't matter. What matters is that you always do the best that you can.'"

George displayed the art for *Independence* where a youth is sitting in thought atop a mountain. "Here I painted a youth on a vision quest. This is a rite of passage where a young person goes out to live alone to discover the purpose of his life. But I didn't find my independence on a vision quest. I found my independence in prison, for this was the first time I could discover who I really could be as a person."

The art portraying *Generosity* was displayed last. George pointed to the grandmother giving soup to hungry children. He explained that the test of generosity was to treat others as relatives. "In my Lakota language, we often say *Mitakuye Oyasin,* which means 'we are all relatives.'"

George concluded by thanking us for allowing him to contribute to this project and took his seat. A sense of awe had captured that prison audience, for they had just been given a homily on the meaning of life from a lifer.

Some years later, in a different political climate, the prison high school curriculum was limited. George no longer is able to teach art and culture to the Native youth who now are being sent into this adult prison. Day after day, he waits as life passes him by. George could not be present when his own father was buried or as his own son began his journey to manhood. Life in prison offers a slim ration of belonging, mastery, independence, and generosity, the components of the Circle of Courage. Since it is easy for George to become discouraged, we chose to write this conclusion to our revised edition in his honor. His contributions are ongoing as the impact of the Circle of Courage spreads.

The authors wrote our original treatise on the Circle of Courage as a summer research project when we were colleagues at Augustana College. In short order, George Blue Bird's powerful Circle of Courage art became the flag for "the reclaiming youth movement," as Linda Lantieri calls it. Here we briefly track the pathway of Reclaiming Youth initiatives sparked by the Circle of Courage philosophy.

The journal *Reclaiming Children and Youth* was founded in 1992 by the authors and Dr. Nicholas Long of American University, with support from Solution Tree (formerly National Educational Service) and Pro-ED publishers. The journal has produced hundreds of practical articles about "strength-based interventions" written by leading experts in work with challenging youth. Compassion Press, an arm of the Crisis Prevention Institute, the world's largest training curriculum in this field, now publishes *Reclaiming Children and Youth*. The journal's mission statement is anchored in the Circle of Courage:

> To network those concerned with reclaiming children and youth in conflict. To reclaim is to restore dignity and courage by providing opportunities for growth in belonging, mastery, independence, and generosity.

The annual *Black Hills Seminars on Reclaiming Youth* was established in 1994, sponsored by the Children's Home Society. This was the vision of Fred Tully, a former troubled youth who became a teacher, therapist, and founder of programs serving troubled children. These seminars draw together professionals, policy leaders, families—all who work on behalf of troubled youth. We gather in the serenity of the Black Hills of South Dakota, which are sacred to tribal peoples of North America.

A highlight of the Black Hills Seminars is the Spirit of Crazy Horse Awards ceremony at Crazy Horse Mountain. Individuals who have made outstanding contributions to building courage in discouraged youth are recognized. Recent honorees include Dr. Dan Olweus of Norway, the world's leading expert on childhood bullying; former U.S. Attorney General Janet Reno for her work on delinquency prevention; Father Chris Riley who founded a network of programs for street youth in Australia; and Linda Lantieri, founder of the Resolving Conflict Creatively program that operates in hundreds of schools in the U.S. and Canada. As the Black Hills Seminars expanded, the non-profit organization Reclaiming Youth International (RYI) was formed in 1997. RYI is involved in research, training, and advocacy initiatives of the reclaiming youth network.

A growing number of researchers and practitioners are using the Circle of Courage model as a basis for new approaches to prevention, treatment, and alternative education. Richard Villa and Jacqueline Thousand employ the Circle of Courage model for inclusion of troubled students.[9] Cathann Kress of Cornell University developed violence prevention models based on the Circle of Courage, which are being disseminated through the 4-H organization.[3] The Life Space Crisis Intervention model of Nicholas Long and colleagues[5] trains front-line professionals in "reclaiming strategies" for communicating with youth in conflict.

Other authors associated with the Reclaiming Youth network are involved in a range of new initiatives. Scott Larson[4] of Straight Ahead Ministries collaborated to create a book on the spiritual development of youth at risk. Eastern Kentucky University turned this book into a web-based course and has produced the video tape series, *Reclaiming Our Prodigal Sons and Daughters*, distributed by Solution Tree (formerly National Educational Service).

The W. K. Kellogg Foundation has funded the Developmental Audit Project, which offers new tools for involving young persons in their assessment and treatment planning. This approach uses problems as opportunities with students creating discipline problems, in treatment planning with troubled youth, and in court cases with difficult delinquents.[7, 10]

A project for developing strategies for "reclaiming unreclaimable kids" is being headed by John Seita of Michigan State University. Seita himself was once a ward of the juvenile court. Today he is a professor of social work and expert on resilience and lead author of the book *Kids Who Outwit Adults*.[6]

At a time when schools and the justice system give up on our most needy youth, Starr Commonwealth has established *No Disposable Kids* training programs. These provide positive strategies for building safe and reclaiming schools. Programs are also available for creating positive peer cultures and healing racism.[1]

Strength-based approaches in treatment and special education for troubled children are the focus of a publication funded by the Allendale Association of Illinois. The Circle of Courage transforms children's mental health from a deficit to a strength-building paradigm.[2]

Long before modern science, First Nations peoples of North America used sophisticated child development strategies designed to nurture caring, respectful, and courageous children. In Lakota culture, children were seen as "sacred beings." Similar concepts come from tribal cultures worldwide. The Maori term for children is translated as "gift of the gods." A Zulu professor of sociology from South Africa describes his culture's respect for children:

> The mere sight of a child touches the very essence of our humanity. A child draws from within us the inclination and instinct for kindness, gentleness, generosity, and love. Accordingly, there is nothing more revolting to our humanity than cruelty to children. These truths we knew at one time and, somehow, subsequently forgot (p. 37).[8]

These concepts arose from cultures that deeply cherished children and treated them with respect and dignity. Now, youth development research has validated these principles of the Circle of Courage:

> **The Spirit of Belonging**: The universal longing for human bonds is cultivated by relationships of trust so that the child can say, "I am loved."
>
> **The Spirit of Mastery**: The inborn thirst for learning is cultivated; by learning to cope with the world, the child can say, "I can succeed."
>
> **The Spirit of Independence**: Free will is cultivated by responsibility so that the child can say, "I have power to make decisions."
>
> **The Spirit of Generosity**: Character is cultivated by concern for others so that the child can say, "I have a purpose for my life."

Belonging, mastery, independence, and generosity are universal human needs. In a society that believes children are sacred beings, these become the birthrights of all of our children.

Full-color prints of the Circle of Courage suitable for framing are available with royalties going to the George Blue Bird Defense Fund. The art displays the Circle of Courage in the center surrounded by the four representations of the points on the Circle. The print is 19" x 28". To order, call toll free 1-888-647-2532 or 1-605-647-2532, Fax: 1-605-647-5212, or write: Circle of Courage, PO Box 57, Lennox, SD 57039. Website: www.reclaiming.com.

# Endnotes

## Introduction

[1]Bronfenbrenner, U. (1979). *The ecology of human development.* Cambridge, MA: Harvard University Press.

[2]Hunt, D. E. (1987). *Beginning with ourselves in practice, theory, and human affairs.* Cambridge, MA: Brookline Books.

[3]Juul, K. (1990). Child and youth care in America and Europe: A history of fruitful mutual influences in special education and therapy. In J. Anglin, C. Denholm, R. V. Ferguson, & A. Pence (Eds.), *Child & Youth Services, 13*(1, 2). Also published in *Perspectives in Professional Child and Youth Care.* New York: Haworth.

[4]Key, E. (1909). *The century of the child.* London: G. P. Putnam's Sons.

[5]Korczak, J. (1967). *Selected works of Janusz Korczak.* Warsaw, Poland: Central Institute for Scientific, Technical and Economic Information.

[6]Mill, J. S. (1869). *The subjection of women.* Arlington Heights, IL: AHM Publishing Company.

[7]Redl, F. (1966). *When we deal with children.* New York: Free Press.

[8]Schorr, L. (1988). *Within our reach: Breaking the cycle of disadvantage.* New York: Doubleday.

[9]Tillich, P. (1952). *The courage to be.* New Haven, CT: Yale University Press.

[10]Wolins, M., & Wozner, Y. (1982). *Revitalizing residential settings: Problems and potential in education, health, rehabilitation and social service.* San Francisco: Jossey-Bass.

## Part I

[1]Ardilo, I. (1979). Con el muchacho de la calle nace una neuva pedagoga [A new pedagogy is born with the child of the street]. *Boletin Salesiano Colombia, 27.* (Translation by Diane Loomis.)

[2]Bacon, S., & Kimball, R. (1989). The wilderness challenge model. In R. Lyman, S. Prentice-Dunn, & S. Gabel (Eds.), *Residential and inpatient treatment of children and adolescents.* New York: Plenum.

[3]Benedict, R. (1938). Continuities and discontinuities in cultural conditioning. *Psychiatry, 1,* 161–167.

[4]Benson, P., Williams, D., & Johnson, A. (1987). *The quicksilver years: The hopes and fears of early adolescence.* San Francisco: Harper & Row.

[5]Brodinsky, B. (1980). *Student discipline: Problems and solutions.* Sacramento, CA: American Association of School Administrators.

[6]Bronfenbrenner, U. (1986). Alienation and the four worlds of childhood. *Phi Delta Kappan, 67,* 430–436.

[7]Brown, W., Miller, T., & Jenkins, R. (1988). The favorable effect of juvenile court adjudication of delinquent youth on first contact with the juvenile system. In R. Jenkins & W. Brown (Eds.), *The abandonment of delinquent behavior.* New York: Praeger.

[8]Charleston, S. (1989). The tyranny of time. *Lutheran Woman Today, 2*(7), 27–32.

[9]Coopersmith, S. (1967). *The antecedents of self-esteem.* San Francisco: W. H. Freeman.

[10]Cullen, F., Larson, M., & Mathers, R. (1985). Having money and delinquent involvement: The neglect of power in delinquency theory. *Criminal Justice and Behavior, 12,* 171–192.

[11]Deal, T. (1985). The symbolism of effective schools. *The Elementary School Journal, 85,* 601–619.

[12]Edelman, M. (1989). Children at risk. *Proceedings of the Academy of Political Science, 27*(2), 20–30.

[13]Empey, L. (1978). *American delinquency: Its meaning and construction.* Homewood, IL: Dorsey Press.

[14]Frankl, V. (1978). *The unheard cry for meaning.* New York: Simon and Schuster.

[15]Gallup, G., & Poling, D. (1980). *The search for America's faith.* Nashville, TN: Abingdon.

[16]Gaycedo, C. (1977). *Colombia Armaga.* Bogotá: Carlos Valencia Editores.

[17]Good, T., & Brophy, J. (1987). *Looking in classrooms.* New York: Harper & Row.

[18]Gordon, T. (1974). *T.E.T.: Teacher effectiveness training.* New York: David McKay.

[19]Greenberger, E., & Steinberg, L. (1986). *When teenagers work: The psychological and social costs of adolescent employment.* New York: Basic Books.

[20]Hamachek, D. (1965). *The self in growth, teaching and learning.* Englewood Cliffs, NJ: Prentice-Hall.

[21]Heider, F. (1958). *The psychology of interpersonal relations.* New York: John Wiley and Sons.

[22]Keith-Lucas, A. (1979). An ethical approach to caring. In *Papers from the Twenty-first Annual Workshop for Personnel of Homes for Children*. Austin: University of Texas.

[23]Menninger, K. (1982). The church's responsibility for the homeless. In R. Gilloghy (Ed.), *Sacred Shelters*. Topeka, KS: The Villages.

[24]Mesinger, J. (1982). Alternative education for behavior disordered and delinquent adolescent youth: What world—Maybe? *Behavioral Disorders, 7,* 91-100.

[25]Miller, W. (1955). Two concepts of authority. *American Anthropologist, 57,* 271–289.

[26]Morse, W. C. (1980). Worksheet on life space interviewing. In N. Long, W. Morse, & R. Newman (Eds.), *Conflict in the classroom* (4th ed.). Belmont, CA: Wadsworth.

[27]National Film Board of Canada (1987). *Richard Cardinal: Cry from the diary of a Metis child* [video]. Montreal, Quebec.

[28]Payne, W. (1875). *Chapters on school supervision*. Cincinnati: Wilson, Hickle.

[29]Phi Delta Kappa Commission on Discipline (1982). *Handbook for developing schools with good discipline*. Bloomington, IN: Phi Delta Kappa.

[30]Regnery, A. (1986). A federal perspective on juvenile justice reform. *Crime and Delinquency, 32*(1), 39–52.

[31]Rich, J., & DeVitis, J. (1985). *Theories of moral development*. Springfield, IL: Charles C. Thomas.

[32]Ross, M. (1976). *The University: The anatomy of academe*. New York: McGraw-Hill, 1976.

[33]Rousseau, J. (1762). *Emile*. Translated by Allan Bloom (1979). New York: Basic Books.

[34]Schorr, L. (1988). *Within our reach: Breaking the cycle of disadvantage.* New York: Doubleday.

[35]Tully, F. (1988). The evolution, devolution, and disruption of treatment of an antisocial child. In R. Jenkins & W. Brown (Eds.), *The abandonment of delinquent behavior.* New York: Praeger.

[36]Turnbull, A., & Turnbull, H. (1978). *Parents speak out.* Columbus, OH: Merrill.

[37]Wallach, M., & Wallach, L. (1983). *Psychology's sanction for selfishness.* San Francisco: W. H. Freeman.

[38]Weiner, B. (1980). A cognitive (attribution)—emotion—action, model of motivated behavior: An analysis of judgements of help-giving. *Journal of Personality and Social Psychology, 39,* 186–200.

[39]Wilson, W. (1987). *The truly disadvantaged.* Chicago: University of Chicago Press.

[40]Wozner, Y. (1985). Institution as community. *Child and Youth Services, 7,* 71–90.

## Part II

[1]Beck, P., & Walters, A. (1977). *The sacred: Ways of knowledge, sources of life.* Tsalie, AZ: Navajo Community College.

[2]Black Elk (1932). *Black Elk speaks.* As told to J. Neihardt. New York: W. Morrow & Co.

[3]Brendtro, L., & Ness, A. (1983). *Re-educating troubled youth.* New York: Aldine.

[4]Bronfenbrenner, U. (1986). Alienation and the four worlds of childhood. *Phi Delta Kappan, 67,* 430–436.

[5]Bryde, J. (1971). *Indian students and guidance.* Boston: Houghton Mifflin.

[6]Carter, F. (1976). *The education of Little Tree.* Albuquerque: University of New Mexico Press.

[7]Collier, J. (1947). *The Indians of the Americas.* New York: W. W. Norton.

[8]Conrad, D., & Hedin, D. (1987). *Youth service.* Washington, DC: Independent Sector.

[9]Coopersmith, S. (1967). *The antecedents of self esteem.* San Francisco: W. H. Freeman.

[10]Deloria, E. C. (1943). *Speaking of Indians.* New York: Friendship Press.

[11]Densmore, F. (1929). *Chippewa customs* (Bureau of American Ethnology Bulletin 86). Washington, DC: Smithsonian Institution.

[12]Eastman, C. (1902). *Indian boyhood.* New York: McClure, Phillips & Co.

[13]Elkind, D. (1984). *All grown up and no place to go.* Reading, MA: Addison-Wesley.

[14]Gauthier, P. (1980). The international year of the child. Youth: Resource or burden. *Residential and Community Child Care Administration, 1,* 337–343.

[15]Giago, T. (1978). *The aboriginal sin.* San Francisco: The Indian Historian Press.

[16]Gilliland, H. (1986). Self concept and the Indian student. In J. Reyhner (Ed.), *Teaching the Indian child.* Billings, MT: Eastern Montana College.

[17]Glasser, W. (1986). *Control theory in the classroom.* New York: Harper & Row.

[18]Goodlad, J. (1984). *A place called school.* New York: McGraw-Hill.

[19]Graff, J. (Ed.) (1987). Strength within the circle. *Journal of Child Care,* special issue.

[20]Haines, E. (1888). *The American Indian.* Chicago: Mas-sin-na-gan Company.

[21]Hassrick, R. (1964). *The Sioux: Life and customs of a warrior society.* Norman: University of Oklahoma Press.

[22]Hoffman, E. (1988). *The right to be human: A biography of Abraham Maslow.* Los Angeles: Jeremy P. Tarcher, Inc.

[23]Hoffman, M. (1977). Moral internalization: Current theory and research. In L. Berkowitz (Ed.), *Advances in Experimental Social Psychology, 10,* New York: Academic Press.

[24]Light, H., & Martin, R. (1985). Guidance of American Indian children: Their heritage and some contemporary views. *Journal of American Indian Education, 25,* 42–46.

[25]Maier, H. (1987). *Developmental group care of children and youth.* New York: The Haworth Press.

[26]Marty, M. (1987). *Religion and republic: The American circumstance.* Boston: Beacon Press.

[27]Menninger, K. (1963). *The vital balance.* New York: Viking Press.

[28]Menninger, K. (1982). The church's responsibility for the homeless. In R. Gillogly (Ed.), *Sacred shelters.* Topeka, KS: The Villages.

[29]Red Bird, S., & Mohatt, G. (1982). *Identity through traditional Lakota Indian methods* (Contract No. MH28697-03). Washington, DC: National Institutes of Mental Health.

[30]Reitz, S. (1986). Preserving Indian culture through oral literature. In J. Reyhner (Ed.) *Teaching the Indian child.* Billings, MT: Eastern Montana College.

[31]Sandoz, M. (1962). *These were the Sioux.* New York: Dell.

[32]Selye, H. (1974). *Stress without distress.* Philadelphia: J. B. Lippincott.

[33]Slavin, R. (1983). *Cooperative learning.* New York: Longman.

[34]Sneve, V. Driving Hawk (1987). Women of the circle. In H. Thompson, A. Huseboe, & S. Looney (Eds.), *A common land, a diverse people.* Sioux Falls, SD: Nordland Heritage Foundation.

[35]Standing Bear, L. (1978 [1933]). *Land of the spotted eagle.* Lincoln: University of Nebraska Press.

[36]Trieschman, A. (1969). Understanding the nature of a therapeutic milieu. In A. Trieschman, J. Whittaker, & L. Brendtro, *The other 23 hours.* New York: Aldine.

[37]Walker, J. (1982). *Lakota society.* Lincoln: University of Nebraska Press.

[38]Warrior, C. (1971). "We are not free." In A. Josephy, Jr. (Ed.), *Red power.* New York: McGraw-Hill.

[39]White, R. (1959). Motivation reconsidered: The concept of competence. *Psychological Review, 66,* 297–333.

[40]Whittaker, J., & Garbarino, J. (1983). *Social support networks.* New York: Aldine.

## Part III

[1]Addams, J. (1909). *The spirit of youth and the city streets.* New York: Macmillan.

[2]Ainsworth, M., Blehar, M., Waters, E., & Wall, S. (1978). *Patterns of attachment: A psychological study of the strange situation.* Hillsdale, NJ: Lawrence Erlbaum Associates.

[3]Bacon, W., & Kimball, R. (1989). The wilderness challenge model. In R. Lyman, S. Prentice-Dunn, & S. Gabel (Eds.),

*Residential and inpatient treatment of children and adolescents.* New York: Plenum.

[4]Batson, C. (1987). Prosocial motivation: Is it ever truly altruistic? *Advances in Experimental Social Psychology, 20,* 65–122.

[5]Benson, P., Williams, D., & Johnson, A. (1987). *The quicksilver years: The hopes and fears of early adolescence.* San Francisco: Harper & Row.

[6]Blom, G., Cheney, B., & Snoddy, J. (1986). *Stress in childhood.* New York: Teachers College Press.

[7]Bowlby, J. (1980). *Attachment and loss, Vol. 3: Loss, sadness and depression.* New York: Basic Books.

[8]Brendtro, L., & Hinders, D. (1990). A saga of Janusz Korczak, the king of children. *Harvard Educational Review, 60*(2).

[9]Brendtro, L., & Ness, A. (1983). *Re-educating troubled youth.* New York: Aldine.

[10]Brendtro, L., Ness, A., & Mitchell, M. (2002). *No disposable kids.* Longmont, CO: Sopris West.

[11]Carnegie Council on Adolescent Development. (1989). *Turning points: Preparing youth for the 21st century.* New York: Carnegie Corporation of New York.

[12]Coles, G. (1987). *The learning mystique.* New York: Pantheon Books.

[13]Combs, A. W. (1982). Affective education or none at all. *Educational Leadership, 39*(7), 495–497.

[14]Conrad, D., & Hedin, D. (1988). *Youth service: A guidebook for developing and operating effective programs.* Washington, DC: The Independent Sector.

[15]Coopersmith, S. (1967). *The antecedents of self-esteem.* San Francisco: W. H. Freeman.

[16]Dreikurs, R. (1982). *Maintaining sanity in the classroom.* New York: Harper & Row.

[17]Durkin, R. (1988). Restructuring for competence: A case for the democratization and communitization of children's programs. In R. Small & F. Alwon (Eds.), *Challenging the limits of care.* Needham, MA: Albert E. Trieschman Center.

[18]Etzioni, A. (1988). *The moral dimension.* New York: The Free Press.

[19]Fromm, E. (1956). *The art of loving.* New York: Harper & Row.

[20]Garner, H. (1988). *Helping others through teamwork: A handbook for professionals.* Washington, DC: Child Welfare League of America.

[21]Glasser, W. (1969). *Schools without failure.* New York: Harper & Row.

[22]Gold, M., & Mann, D. (1984). *Expelled to a friendlier place: A study of effective alternative schools.* Ann Arbor: University of Michigan Press.

[23]Hall, G. S. (1904). *Adolescence (Vols. I & II).* New York: Appleton.

[24]Hall, G. S. (1829). *Lectures on school-keeping.* Boston: Richardson, Lord and Holbrook.

[25]Harris, A. J., & Simpay, E. R. (1985). *How to increase reading ability* (8th ed.). New York: Longman.

[26]Hart, L. A. (1983). *Human brain and human learning.* New York: Longman.

[27]Hedin, D. (1989). The power of community service. *Proceedings of the Academy of Political Science, 37*(2), 201–213.

[28]Help for at-risk kids. (June 26, 1989). *Time, 51.*

[29]Hemming, J. (1980). *The betrayal of youth*. Boston: Marian Boyars.

[30]Hobbs, N. (1982). *The troubled and troubling child*. San Francisco: Jossey-Bass.

[31]Iole, M., & Dolan, A. (1989). *Caring, commitment, and courage: Empowering children to help others*. Trieschman award-winning paper. Needham, MA: Albert E. Trieschman Center.

[32]James, W. (1984). The moral equivalent of war. In B. Wilshire (Ed.), *William James: The essential writings*. Albany: State University of New York Press.

[33]Jenkins, R. (1945). The constructive use of punishment. *Mental Hygiene, 29*, 561–574.

[34]Johnson, R., Johnson, D., & Stanne, M. B. (1986). Comparison of computer-assisted cooperative, competitive, and individualistic learning. *American Educational Research Journal 23*(3), 382–392.

[35]Keith-Lucas, A. (1980). The foundations of caring. *Papers from the Twenty-first Annual Workshop for Personnel of Homes for Children*. Austin: University of Texas.

[36]Konopka, G. (1985). A renewed look at human development, human needs, human services. *Proceedings of the Annual Gisela Konopka Lectureship*. St. Paul: University of Minnesota Center for Youth Development and Research.

[37]Korczak, J. (1967). *Selected works of Janusz Korczak*. Warsaw, Poland: Central Institute for Scientific, Technical and Economic Information.

[38]Korczak, J. (1986). *King Matt the First*. New York: Farrar, Straus and Giroux.

[39]Lerner, R., & Galambos, N. (1984). *Experiencing adolescents.* New York: Garland Publishing Company.

[40]Lifton, B. (1988). *The king of children: A biography of Janusz Korczak.* New York: Farrar, Straus and Giroux.

[41]Long, N., Morse, W., & Newman, R. (1980). *Conflict in the classroom* (4th ed.). Belmont, CA: Wadsworth.

[42]Loughmiller, C. (1978). *Kids in trouble.* Tyler, TX: Wildwood Books.

[43]Lozanov, G. (1978). *Suggestology and outline of suggestopedy.* New York: Gordon and Breach.

[44]Maier, H. (1987). *Developmental group care of children.* New York: Haworth Press.

[45]Matza, D. (1987). Position and behavior patterns of youth. In H. Graff (Ed.), *Growing up in America.* Detroit: Wayne State University Press.

[46]McClelland, D. (1973). Sources of an achievement. In D. McClelland & R. Steele (Eds.), *Human motivation.* Morristown, NJ: General Learning Press.

[47]Mitchell, M., & Ameen, C. (1989). Program evaluation: A blueprint for excellence. In E. Balcerzak (Ed.), *Group care of children: Transition toward the year 2000.* Washington, DC: Child Welfare League of America.

[48]Murphy, L. (1987). Further reflections on resilience. In E. Anthony & B. Cohler (Eds.), *The invulnerable child.* New York: Guilford Press.

[49]Osgood, D., Gruber, E., Archer, M., & Newcomb, T. (1985). Autonomy for inmates: Counterculture or cooptation? *Criminal Justice and Behavior, 12,* 71–89.

[50]Overly, N. V. (Ed.) (1979). *Lifetime learning.* Alexandria, VA: Association of Supervision and Curriculum Development.

[51]Parkes, C., & Stevenson-Hinde, J. (1982). *The place of attachment in human behavior.* New York: Basic Books.

[52]Peck, M. (1978). *The road less travelled.* New York: Simon and Schuster.

[53]Pestalozzi, J. (1951). *The education of man: Aphorisms.* New York: Philosophical Library.

[54]Pestalozzi, J. (1980). Letter dated 1799 from Pestalozzi to a friend concerning his orphanage at Stans. In R. de Guimps (Ed.), *Pestalozzi: His life and work.* New York: Appleton.

[55]Powell, N. (1989). The conflict cycle model. In M. Krueger & N. Powell (Eds.), *Choices in caring: Contemporary approaches to child and youth care work.* Washington, DC: Child Welfare League of America.

[56]Raychaba, B. (1988). *To be on our own.* Canadian National Youth in Care Network. Ottawa: Runge Press.

[57]Redl, F. (1952). *Controls from within.* New York: Free Press.

[58]Richards, A. (1981). *Kurt Hahn: The midwife of educational ideas.* Doctoral thesis, University of Colorado.

[59]Slavin, R. (1982). *Cooperative learning: Student teams.* Washington, DC: National Education Association.

[60]Smith, F. (1986). *Insult to intelligence.* New York: Arbor House.

[61]Thomas, G. (1989). Keeping children's needs paramount: A new era of accountability and opportunity for group residential services. *Child and Youth Quarterly, 18,* 81–92.

[62]Vorrath, H., & Brendtro, L. (1985). *Positive peer culture* (2nd ed.). New York: Aldine.

[63]Wasmund, W. (1988). The social climates of peer group and other residential programs. *Child and Youth Care Quarterly, 17,* 146–155.

[64]White, R. (1959). Motivation reconsidered: The concept of competence. *Psychological Review, 66,* 297–333.

[65]Whittaker, J. (1979). *Caring for troubled children.* San Francisco: Jossey-Bass.

[66]Wiggington, E. (1986). *Sometimes a shining moment: The fox-fire experience.* Garden City, NY: Anchor Books.

[67]Wolfe, J. (1988). Adolescent suicide—An open letter to counselors. *Phi Delta Kappan, 70,* 294–295.

[68]Wood, F. (1986). Special education for disturbed adolescents. In S. Apter & A. Goldstein (Eds.), *Youth violence: Programs and prospects.* New York: Pergamon Press.

## Afterword

[1]Brendtro, L., Ness, A., & Mitchell, M. (2002). *No disposable kids.* Longmont, CO: Sopris West.

[2]Brendtro, L. K., & Shahbazian, M. (2002). *With respect to troubled kids.* Longmont, CO: Sopris West.

[3]Kress, C., & Randall, H. K., (Eds.). (1998). *BOOMERANG! Character Education Program.* Prepared by Brenda Ranum, Cindy Baumgartner, and Vanette Grover, 4-H Youth Development, Iowa State University Extension.

[4]Larson, S., & Brendtro, L. (2000). *Reclaiming our prodigal sons and daughters.* Bloomington, IN: Solution Tree (formerly National Educational Service).

[5]Long, N. J., Fecser, F. A., & Wood, M. M. (2001). *Life space crisis intervention.* Austin, TX: Pro-ED.

[6]Seita, J. R., & Brendtro, L. K. (2002). *Kids who outwit adults.* Longmont, CO: Sopris West.

[7]Van Bockern, S., & Brendtro, L. K. (2002). *Developmental audit project.* Sioux Falls, SD: Reclaiming Youth International, Augustana College.

[8]Vilakazi, H. (1993). Rediscovering lost truths. *Journal of Emotional and Behavioral Problems, 1*(4) 37.

[9]Villa, R. A., & Thousand, J. S. (2000). *Restructuring for caring and effective education: Piecing the puzzle together (2nd ed.).* Baltimore: Paul H. Brookes.

[10]Wood, M. M., Brendtro, L. K., Fecser, F. A., & Nichols, P. (1999). *Psychoeducation: An idea whose time has come.* [Monograph in a series edited by Lyndal M. Bullock & Robert A. Gable.] Reston, VA: Council for Children with Behavioral Disorders.

# Index

## A

Achievement motivation. *See* Motivation
Addams, Jane, 17, 18, 108, 119
Adult domination, 93
Adventure education, 99, 114–115
Affection, 93
Aggression, 28, 30
Aichorn, August, 24
Alienation, 5, 8
Allendale Association of Illinois, 136
Altruism, 120–122
American Association of School Administrators, 31
Ashton-Warner, Sylvia, 15
"At risk," concept of, 3
Attachment, 72–75
Attention deficit disorder, 97–98
Attribution theory, 20
Authority, 25–26, 31–32
Autonomy. *See* Independence

## B

Batson, C., 121, 122
Behavior, theories of, 20–24
Belleroe, Eddie, 59
Belonging, 4, 45
    Blue Bird on, 133
    characteristics of, 62
    children without, 12–14
    in schools, 86–88
    spirit of, 46–48, 137
Benedict, Ruth, 25
Blackfoot Indians, 53

Blue Bird, George, 45, 131–134, 138
Blue Whirlwind, 54
Boaz, Franz, 66
Boredom, 17
Bosconia La Florida, 26
Brain
    pattern-making, 94–96
    threatened, 95–98
    *See also* Learning
Brain-friendly learning. *See* Learning
Brendtro, L., 59
Bronfenbrenner, Urie, 2, 7
Business management theory, 40–41

## C

Canon, Carlos, 26
Capital punishment. *See* Punishment
Cardinal, Richard, 9–11
Caregivers, youth as, 4
Caring, 70, 119–120
    altruism, 120–122
    curriculum for, 123–128
    fashionable, 113–114
Carnegie Council on Adolescent Development, 123
Casing, 80
Charleston, Steve, 39
Child-rearing, 28–33
    Native American, 43–45
Circle of Courage
    artist George Blue Bird, 45, 131–138
    users of, 135–136

*See also* Belonging; Generosity; Independence; Mastery
Climates of futility. *See* Futility
Cognition, 21–23
Coles, Gerald, 95
Collier, John, 43
Community, responsibility of, 12
Community service, 38–39, 59, 123
    *See also* Service learning
Competence. *See* Mastery
Competence motivation. *See* Motivation
Conflict cycle, 79
Consequences, natural, 110
Cooperative learning, 100–101
Coopersmith, Stanley, 44, 107
Corporal punishment. *See* Punishment
Courage
    to care, 70, 119–130
    denied, 61–66
    *See also* Circle of Courage
Crisis, 76–78

## D

Delinquency, 29
Deloria, Ella, 46, 50, 66
De Montaigne, Michel, 91
De Nicolo, Javier, 26
Destructive relationships, 8, 9–14
Developmental Audit Project, 136
Deviance, 19–20
Discipline
    punishment compared with, 109–111
    for responsibility, 70, 103–118
Discouragement, 61
Disempowerment, 107–108
Dix, Dorothea, 129
Dolan, Anne, 126, 127
Domination, adult, 93

Dreikurs, R., 110
Dubois, W.E.B, 25
Durkin, Roderick, 104

## E

Eastman, C., 57
Eckerd Wilderness Educational System, 99
Edelman, Marian Wright, 34
Education. *See* Schools
*Education of Little Tree, The,* 57, 60
Einstein, Albert, 97
Elkind, D., 59
Empathy, 121–122
Employment. *See* Work
English explorers, 31–32
Etzioni, Amitia, 120
Europeans, 31–32
Expectations, 16, 93
Experiential learning, 98–99

## F

Failure, 93–94
Family
    tribe compared with, 12
    *See also* Parents
Foxfire, 99
Frankl, Victor, 34
Freedom
    with self control, 107–118
    *See also* Independence
French explorers, 31–32
Fromm, Eric, 76
Futility, 8, 15–24
Future citizens, 17, 25

## G

Gallup, George Jr., 17
Games, 50, 85
Gangs, 25, 26–28, 114
Garfat, Thomas, 15

Garner, Howard, 89
Gaycedo, Castro, 27
Generosity
    Blue Bird on, 132
    characteristics of, 65
    spirit of, 57–59, 135
*Ghetto Diary,* 69, 130
Gibran, Kahlil, 35
Giving. *See* Generosity
Glasser, W., 55, 93
Goethe, 24
Greatness, 112–113
Greenberger, E., 36

# H

Hahn, Kurt, 17, 37, 115, 123–124
Haines, Elijah, 53–54
Hall, G. Stanley, 17, 119
Hall, G. Samuel, 76
Hart, Leslie, 94
Heider, F., 20
Hemingway, Ernest, 94
Hobbs, Nicholas, 73, 81, 85, 92
Hoffman, M., 55
Howe, Harold II, 25
Human behavior, 20–24
Hunt, David, 2

# I

Independence, 93
    characteristics of, 64
    profile of, 104–107
    spirit of, 52–56, 138
    *See also* Freedom
Indulgence, 28–30
Inner cities, 13
Iole, Michelle, 126, 127
Irresponsibility. *See* Learned
    irresponsibility
Itard, Jean Marc, 15, 129

# J

James, William, 17, 119
Jenkins, Richard, 110
Jobs. *See* Work
Joy, 85–86

# K

Keith-Lucas, Alan, 120
Kellogg Foundation, 136
Key, Ellen, 1, 5, 130
*King Matt the First,* 108
Konopka, Gisela, 103
Korczak, Janusz, 5–6, 69–70, 74, 98
    adult/child relationships, 07–108
    Nazi death camp, 129–130
Kress, Cathann, 135

# L

Labels, 7, 23
    relabeling, 114
Lantieri, Linda, 134–135
Larson, Scott, 136
Leadership, youth, 116–117
Leadership relationships, 90
Learned helplessness, 25
Learned irresponsibility, 8, 17,
    25–33
    profile in discouragement, 26–28
    tyranny of indulgence, 28–30
    tyranny of obedience, 30–33
    *See also* Responsibility
Learners club, 99–100
Learning
    achievement and, 92–94
    brain-friendly, 70, 91–102
    cooperative, 100–101
    experiential, 98–99
    nonthreatening, 95–98
    pattern-making, 94–95
    service, 123–128
    social, 99–102

Learning disabled, 95
Life space, 82–84
Life Space Crisis Intervention
    (LSCI), 83–84, 136
Limit testing, 80
Little Tree. *See Education of Little
    Tree, The*
Long, Nicholas, 79, 83, 134, 136
Lorang, Tom, 87
Loss of purpose. *See* Purpose, loss of
Loughmiller, Campbell, 99
Louis XIII (France), 29

# M

Maier, H., 55–56
Management theory, 40–41
Mann, Horace, 16, 129
Markham, Edwin, 71, 88
Marty, Martin, 12, 47
Maslow, Abraham, 23, 53
Mastery, 4, 45
    achievement motivation, 92–94
    Blue Bird on, 133
    characteristics of, 63
    spirit of, 49–51, 135, 137
Materialism, 35
McClelland, David, 92
Meade, Margaret, 66
Menninger, Karl, 9, 48, 66
Mill, John Stuart, 2
Miller, Walter, 31
Modeling, 74
Montessori, Maria, 15
Morse, William, 84
Motivation
    achievement, 49, 92–93
    competence, 49, 50, 92

# N

Narcissism, 25, 35, 65, 125
Native Americans

child-rearing, 43–45, 133–134
    obedience, 32
Natural consequences, 110
Negative environments, 16
Negative expectations, 16
Negative labels, 21*t*, 23
Ness, A., 59
*No Disposable Kids,* 136

# O

Obedience
    achievement motivation and, 93
    greatness instead of, 112–113
    training, 25, 31–33
O'Gorman High School, 86–88
Olweus, Dr. Dan, 135
Omaha, peer programs, 117
Outward Bound. *See* Hahn, Kurt
Ownership, 112

# P

Parenting. *See* Child-rearing
Parents, 14
    teamwork relationships, 89
    teenage, 29
    *See also* Family
Pathway School, 126
Pattern-making, 94–95
Payne, William, 40
Peck, M. Scott, 122
Peer-group relationships, 88
Peer subcultures. *See* Subcultures
Peers, power of, 26, 116–118
Pessimism, 15, 17–20
Pestalozzi, Johann, 15, 16, 98, 119,
    129
Play, 50
Positive labels, 22*t*, 23
Power, 45
Predictability, 80
Pseudo-altruism, 121–122

Punishment, 16–17
    corporal and capital, 24
    discipline compared with, 109–111
    Native Americans and, 54–55
    in schools, 31
Punitiveness. *See* Punishment
Purpose
    depersonalization of education,
        40–41
    loss of, 8, 34–41
    misery of unimportance, 37–40
    work without meaning, 35–37
Pygmalion effect, 16

# R

Rebellion, 25, 26
Reclaiming, concepts of, 3–4, 69–70
    *See also* specific concept
Redl, Fritz, 1, 78, 82, 83, 88, 111
Relabeling, 114
Relationship-resistance, 9
Relationships, 71–72
    attachment, 72–75
    building, 75–88
    destructive, 8, 9–14
    reluctant, 70, 71–72
    synergistic, 88–90
Relationship technology, 75–88
Reno, Janet, 135
Respect, 84–85
Responsibility
    community, 12
    demanding, 112
    discipline for, 70, 103–118
    reverse, 112–113
    *See also* Learned irresponsibility
Reward, 54–55
Riley, Chris, 135
Rousseau, Jean Jacques, 14, 25–26,
    28, 32–33, 107, 110
Rules, 111

# S

Schools, 4
    belonging in, 86–88
    codes of conduct, 31
    corporal punishment in, 24
    depersonalization of, 40–41
    failure of, 13
    professionals, 14
    selfish strategies in, 35
    as "tribes," 12
Schorr, Lisbeth, 4
Seita, John, 136
Self-control, freedom with, 107–118
Self-esteem
    components of, 44–45
Selfishness, 34–35
Selye, Hans, 59
Service learning, 123–125
    projects, 126–128
    *See also* Community service
Sexual abuse, 29–30
Shakespeare, William, 34
Significance, 45
Simplicity, 60
Smith, Frank, 99
Sneve, Virginia Driving Hawk, 60
Social psychology, 20–23
Social reinforcement, 74
Staff teamwork relationships, 89
Standing Bear, 46, 49, 54–55
Starr Commonwealth Schools, 90,
    136
Starr, Floyd, 18, 80
Steinberg, L., 36
Stories, 49–50
Subcultures
    language of, 113–114
    peer, 26
    *See also* Gangs
Success. *See* Mastery
Supreme Court. *See* United States
    Supreme Court

## T

Teenage parents, 29
Terence (Roman philosopher), 122
Therapy on the hoof, 82–84
Thomas, George, 75
Thousand, Jacqueline, 135
Threats, 95–98
Time, concept of, 39–40
Tribes, 12–13, 46
Trieschman, Albert, 54, 72
Trust, 79–81
Tully, F., 29–30, 135

## U

Unimportance, misery of, 37–40
United States Supreme Court, 24

## V

Verbal intervention, 114
Villa, Richard, 135
Virtue, 45

Volunteer work. *See* Community service

## W

W. K. Kellogg Foundation, 136
Wandervogel youth movement, 24
Warrior, Clyde, 52
*When Teenagers Work,* 36
White, Robert, 49, 92
Wilderness programs, 99, 115
Wilson, William Julius, 13
Wolins, Martin, 3–4, 69
Work
    community service, 38–39, 59, 123
    Native American children, 50
    without meaning, 36–37
Wozner, Yochanan, 41

## Z

Zirker, Otto, 106

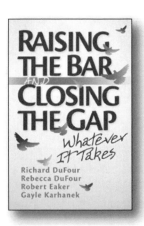

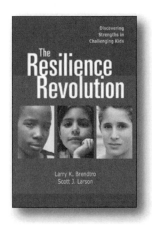

### Raising the Bar and Closing the Gap
*Richard DuFour, Rebecca DuFour, Robert Eaker, and Gayle Karhanek*
This sequel to the best-selling *Whatever It Takes: How Professional Learning Communities Respond When Kids Don't Learn* expands on original ideas and presses further with new insights. **BKF378**

### The Resilience Revolution
*Larry K. Brendtro and Scott J. Larson*
Discover effective ways of connecting with youth at risk. In this inspiring resource, the authors focus on strength-based alternatives to punishment. **BKF210**

### From Rage to Hope
*Crystal Kuykendall*
*Foreword by Asa G. Hilliard III*
Get an authentic view of the academic underachievement, apathy, and rage among America's Black and Hispanic youth and discover how you can become a Merchant of Hope. **BKF157**

### Reclaiming Youth at Risk
*Larry K. Brendtro, Martin Brokenleg, and Steve Van Bockern*
Venture inside schools that have successfully reached youth at risk. Set includes three 20-minute DVDs and a facilitator's guide. **DVF011**

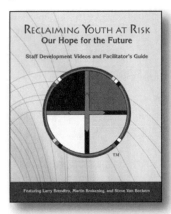

# Solution Tree | Press

*a division of*
Solution Tree

Visit www.solution-tree.com or call 800.733.6786 to order.